Ella D. Curry

Welcome to Soignée Lifestyle Magazine

Dive into the pages of Soignée Lifestyle Magazine and immerse yourself in a space that goes beyond the surface, challenging stereotypes and carving a space where authenticity and grace reign supreme. Join us as we celebrate the elegance of the Soignée Sisterhood — a refined space where individual uniqueness is not only celebrated but revered.

Our mission is clear: to provide a sanctuary where Black women can express their truths, collectively enhancing the strength of women of color and recognizing our joint influence.

So, let this magazine be a force that shapes your individual journeys and contributes to a universe where empowerment knows no bounds. Thank you for joining us on this journey! Here's to the Soignée Sisterhood and the stories that echo through lives and beyond. Please share this magazine with other sister-friends, too!

CONTENT

03 Celebrating Our Sisters

- Black Women's History Month
- Reclaiming Femininity and Redefining Feminism
- Loving Me More
- Just Let Me Be

10 Possibilities Beyond Limits

- Essential Wellness: Habits for Balance and Harmony
- A Right Worthy Woman: A Novel by Ruth P. Watson
- Double Lives by Mary Monroe
- Women of the Post by Joshunda Sanders

19 Legacy: Our Stories

- Women of the Post by Joshunda Sanders
- Saving Raine by Marian L. Thomas
- The Heart and Soul of Black Women by Janet Autherine
- Wild Heart, Peaceful Soul by Janet Autherine

30 Written For Us—By Us

- No Reservations: A Novel of Friendship by Sheryl Lister
- Preying Time Trilogy by Tracie Loveless Hill
- A Passionate Mind in Relentless Pursuit by Noliwe Rooks
- Emancipation's Daughters by Riché Richardson

42 Testimonies Loading

- Daisy: Between a Rock and a Hard Place by Janis F. Kearney
- From Rights to Lives: Evolution of the Black Freedom Struggle
- Beyond the Black Lady: Sexuality and African American Middle Class

Photo of Daisy Lee Bates, Arkansas NAACP president, 1957. Photo Courtesy University of Arkansas Libraries (MC 582, Daisy Bates Papers, Box 9, Picture 6). Cover Photo by Kenilev Terku from Pexel: @kenilev_photographer. Other stock photos are from Pixistock, Envato Elements, Unsplash, and Pexels. Thank you for allowing such amazing artists to share their creations with other content creators.

CONTENT

49   **Truth to Power**

- #SayHerName: Black Women's Stories of Police Violence
- Sister, Are You Ready To Tap-in?
- Surviving Life's Punches: When Everything Sucks
- Embracing Your Season: Soignée Womanhood

64   **Empowered and Flourishing**

- Nourish Your Mind, Body, and Soul Spiritually
- Triumph Over Self-Sabotage
- Embrace Your Tribe
- Boss Babe Blueprint: Dominate Your Online Boutique

76   **Embrace Your Tribe**

- A Millennial's Guide to Smart Money Moves
- How We Love, Heal & Empower
- Unlocking Self-Discovery
- Embrace Freedom: The Art of Letting Go

91   **Renew, Recharge and Revive**

- Prioritizing Self-Care During Menopause
- Healing, Finances, and Inner Renewal
- Soignée Soul After Dark
- Unleashing Your Inner Badass

107   **Be the Magic**

- Embracing Your Beautiful Imperfections
- Soignée Soul Journal Prompts
- Connect Beyond the Pages!
- Showcase Your Gifts with EDC Creations

Ella D. Curry, President of Crown Holders Transmedia

In this latest issue of Soignée Lifestyle Magazine, we delve into the stories and insights of African American women authors and the womanist movement.

Soignée Lifestyle Magazine celebrates International Black Women's History Month by honoring the achievements and legacies of Black women globally. Through amplifying voices, fostering solidarity, and advocating for equity, we recognize their pivotal role in shaping society.

This month-long celebration reminds us of the resilience, strength, and unwavering commitment to justice and equality that Black women embody.

As we commemorate their remarkable contributions, let us also reflect on the lessons learned, the memories cherished in their music, art work, poetry, cookbooks, and autobiographies, and the values instilled along the paths they opened for all women. Their legacy as writers and leaders will endure in the hearts and minds of all who have been part of their journey.

Join us in honoring the past and shaping the future with the written word! Let's continue the fight for a more inclusive and equitable world. Together, we can amplify the voices of women leaders, foster solidarity with the underserved, and advocate for lasting change.

So, let's unite to celebrate the enduring legacy of the women we featured for International Black Women's History Month and commit ourselves to building a brighter tomorrow for all.

International Black Women's History Month is dedicated to Black women's resilience, triumphs, and contributions worldwide. It is an opportunity to celebrate and raise awareness of these remarkable women's invaluable role in shaping our societies, cultures, and futures.

International Black Women's History Month is more than a mere commemoration; it's a call to action, a celebration of strength, and a commitment to amplifying voices often marginalized. It's an opportunity to honor the multifaceted identities and experiences within the Black community and recognize that diversity is the cornerstone of progress.

To celebrate, we must first acknowledge and honor the contributions of Black women authentically. Let's lift their achievements from the shadows, highlighting their groundbreaking accomplishments in every sphere of life. From science to politics, art to activism, their impact reverberates through time, shaping our collective narrative.

Amplification is key! We must provide space for Black women to freely tell their stories, express their perspectives, and discuss visions for the future. We create space for meaningful dialogue and transformative change by actively listening and valuing their voices.

Empowerment lies in education. Take the time to delve into Black women's history, from the unsung heroes to the trailblazers who paved the way. By understanding their struggles and triumphs, we equip ourselves with the knowledge to dismantle systemic barriers and champion equity and inclusion.

Support is solidarity. Show your commitment by patronizing Black women-owned businesses, advocating for economic opportunities, and lifting each other up. Solidarity is our strength; together, we can create pathways to success for all.

Above all, let us remember that celebrating Black women's history extends far beyond the confines of a single month. It's a lifelong commitment to justice, equality, and empowerment. So, as we honor the legacy of past generations, let us pledge to continue the fight—not just in April but every day of the year.

By honoring Black women, we honor humanity's resilience, creativity, and boundless potential. Together, let's build a future where every voice is heard, every dream is realized, and every woman —regardless of race, culture, creed, or background—can thrive.

RECLAIMING
Femininity

Redefining
Feminism
Black Women's
Perspectives

Reclaiming Femininity and Redefining Feminism: Black Women's Perspectives

Black women stand at the intersection of multiple identities and experiences, shaping their own narratives and definitions in the ongoing dialogue surrounding feminism and femininity. Beyond the historical waves of feminism, which have often been dominated by the experiences and perspectives of white women, Black women have been crafting their own movements and ideologies that speak directly to their unique challenges and aspirations.

Black women's journey to reclaim femininity is deeply intertwined with the broader struggle for equality and liberation. It involves challenging societal expectations and stereotypes and embracing the full spectrum of their identities, from their physical appearance to their cultural heritage. Black femininity is not constrained by narrow definitions; it encompasses strength, resilience, and authenticity in the face of systemic oppression.

As Black women navigate their experiences' complexities, they have forged their own paths within the feminist movement. Womanism reflects a holistic approach to feminism that centers on Black women's experiences and acknowledges the interconnectedness of race, gender, and class. Within this framework, Black women have been at the forefront of advocating for issues that are often overlooked or marginalized within mainstream feminism, such as reproductive justice, intersectionality, and the fight against racial and gender-based violence.

What is a Womanist?
A womanist (coined by Alice Walker in her book In Search of Our Mothers' Gardens: Womanist Prose, where she speaks out as a Black woman, writer, mother, and feminist) is unlike traditional feminism, womanism centers on the lived experiences of African American women, addressing issues such as violence, pay disparity, and underrepresentation in media and politics. Through this movement, womanists challenge systemic oppression globally, advocating for the liberation and empowerment of all genders within the Black community.

While celebrating all women, the womanist remains dedicated to fostering the survival and thriving of both genders. They envision a world where men and women can peacefully coexist while preserving their unique cultural identities. This inclusive stance offers Black women a platform to confront gender-based oppression without resorting to direct attacks on men, often advocating for and defending men in the process.

Can You Be a Womanist and a Feminist?
While womanism and feminism share common goals of gender equality and social justice, their approaches and focus differ. Feminism traditionally has been critiqued for primarily representing the concerns and experiences of white, middle-class women. In contrast, womanism embraces a more inclusive and intersectional perspective, centering the experiences of Black women and acknowledging the interconnectedness of race, gender, and class.

Reclaiming Femininity and Redefining Feminism: Black Women's Perspectives

Despite these differences, many individuals identify with both womanism and feminism, recognizing the importance of addressing gender-based oppression while also acknowledging the unique struggles faced by Black women. Ultimately, the identification as a womanist, feminist, or a combination of both is contingent upon individual convictions, life experiences, and the emphasis placed on promoting gender equality and social justice.

In essence, reclaiming femininity for Black women is not simply about conforming to societal expectations or ideals; it is about asserting their agency, embracing their identity, and reshaping the narrative on their own terms. By centering their experiences and perspectives, Black women are not only redefining femininity but also reshaping the landscape of feminism itself, paving the way for a more inclusive and equitable future for all.

What Does Femininity Mean to Black Women?
Femininity for Black women transcends superficial appearances; it encompasses resilience, strength, and individuality. It's about celebrating diverse experiences and rewriting narratives that have historically marginalized us. So, Black women, what does femininity mean to you?

Four Empowering Steps for Women to Embrace Femininity

1. Embrace Authenticity: Reclaiming femininity involves embracing your authentic self, including all aspects of your identity, appearance, and personality. Reject societal norms and stereotypes that dictate how women should look or behave, and instead celebrate your uniqueness and individuality.

2. Challenge Traditional Gender Roles: Break free from traditional gender roles that limit women's opportunities and potential. Assert your agency by pursuing interests and activities that resonate with your passions and aspirations, regardless of whether they align with traditional notions of femininity.

3. Cultivate Self-Compassion: Practice self-compassion and self-care as essential to reclaiming femininity. Prioritize your physical, mental, and emotional well-being, recognizing that vulnerability and imperfection are inherent parts of the human experience.

4. Foster Sisterhood and Support: Build strong connections with other women and foster a sense of sisterhood and solidarity. Create spaces where women can uplift and empower each other, share experiences and insights, and collectively work towards dismantling patriarchal systems of oppression.

01
Soignée

Loving Me More

Just Let Me Be

Imagine how much happier we would be, how much freer to be our true individual selves, if we didn't have the weight of gender expectations." — Chimamanda Ngozi Adichie

Imagine a world where societal expectations on gender are lifted, allowing us to embrace unparalleled happiness and freedom. The journey of a Black woman unfolds, characterized by her remarkable resilience, showcasing immense strength in the face of challenges.

In the midst of adversity, laughter becomes a mirror reflecting an unyielding spirit, while trust emerges as a formidable force, conquering doubt. Love, an enduring source of strength, withstands the scars of the past.

The narrative of a Black woman defies predefined assurances, finding definition in the lived reality of determined perseverance. Through the synergy of laughter, trust, and love, she transforms her story, celebrating endurance and triumph.

A powerhouse, she stands as a beacon of success, unyielding in her own truths without society's validation. Her passion shapes the unfolding chapters of her untold journey, inviting the world to witness her unwavering strength. Just let her be! Allow her to evolve. She is me!

Go Be Great

Igniting Your Possibilities Beyond Limits!
When your dreams outgrow where you are, honey, it's time to find your own reminders that there's more out there. Don't let the fear of your own success hold you back because you deserve the best life, right now! The world is bigger than you can even imagine.

Now, as you reflect on the vastness of your dreams, consider these questions: What is calling you to step into uncharted territory and embrace the vastness that lies beyond? Where do your dreams yearn to break free from your current confines? What is your purpose?

Reflect on Your Desires!
Jot down your dreams. Which visions feel too grand for your present circumstances? What needs to happen to make this reachable? Writing out your vision clarifies your aspirations and serves as a potent reminder of the grandeur within you. Your dreams are too expansive to be confined by your current spaces! Go be great, sis! Embrace the greatness calling your name, and witness the universe unfold its limitless possibilities for you!

Embrace your gifts, grace, and sophistication because you are now a SoignéeWoman! Navigate the world with timeless style and poise, letting your every gesture exude confidence. Go out there and be great—your presence is destined to leave an indelible mark. You've got this!

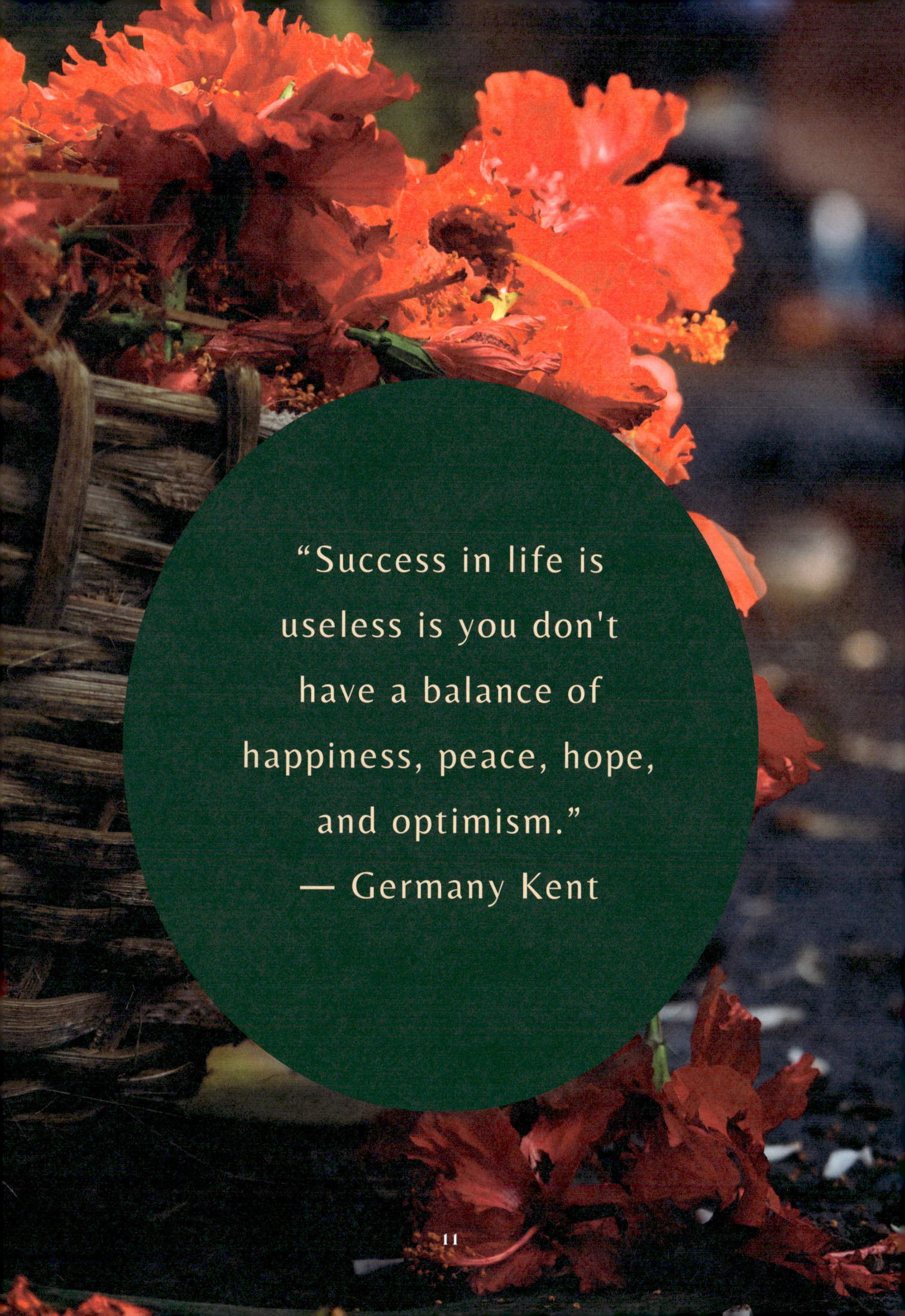

"Success in life is useless is you don't have a balance of happiness, peace, hope, and optimism."
— Germany Kent

Loving Me More: Essential Wellness Habits for Balance and Harmony

It's easy to lose sight of what truly matters when it comes to our health and well-being, especially when our lives are filled with tough choices and an overflowing to-do list. Amidst the hustle and bustle, we must ground ourselves and prioritize our health and happiness. Join us as we delve into powerful practices that integrate seamlessly into our daily routines, fostering equilibrium amidst the chaos.

Empower Yourself with Self-Care: Make self-care a non-negotiable part of your daily routine. This is more than just a buzzword; it's a powerful tool that allows you to honor your needs, set boundaries, and make time for activities that nourish your body, mind, and soul.

Mindful Eating: Cultivate an intentional approach to eating by savoring each bite, paying attention to hunger and fullness cues, and choosing nourishing foods that fuel your body. Eating mindfully promotes better digestion and nutrient absorption and fosters a deeper connection to the food we eat and its importance for our bodies.

Quiet Your Mind: Amidst the whirlwind of daily routines, deliberately pausing your thoughts can wield profound transformation. Embrace mindfulness and meditation, uncomplicated yet potent practices that anchor you to the present, alleviating stress and fostering tranquility. Through these routines, a journey to heightened self-awareness begins, enhancing concentration and cultivating a serene perspective.

Slowing Down: In a world that often values busyness, slowing down can be a radical act of self-care. It's about taking time daily to pause, breathe, and appreciate the present moment. This could be as simple as taking a few deep breaths before you leave your car or as indulgent as scheduling a regular facial and massage or total spa day. Whether it's savoring a new audiobook, going for a leisurely stroll, or simply sitting in silence, slowing down can help calm the mind and reduce stress.

Managing Anxiety: When feelings of anxiety or overwhelm arise, it's important to have tools to help manage them effectively. Take a few moments for yourself to practice deep breathing, journaling, or mindfulness meditation. Alongside these practices, consider integrating soothing physical movements such as yoga or tai chi into your routine. Engaging in hobbies or activities that bring you joy and relaxation can also provide a sense of calm. Finally, remind yourself that it's okay to take breaks and step away from stressors when needed, allowing yourself the time and space to recharge and regain perspective.

Seeking Support: Don't be afraid to reach out for support when you need it. Whether it's talking to a trusted friend, seeking guidance from a therapist or church counselor, or joining a niche support group, reaching out for help is a sign of strength, not weakness. Surround yourself with a supportive network of people who lift you up and encourage your growth.

Loving Me More: Essential Wellness Habits for Balance and Harmony

Set Realistic Goals: This is about breaking down big tasks into smaller, more manageable steps. It's about setting yourself up for success by setting achievable and realistic goals. By doing this, you can achieve incremental victories and celebrate milestones along the way. This systematic approach can propel your progress and instill lasting positivity, invigorating your mood and ultimately leading to a more triumphant pursuit of your objectives.

Socialize: Cultivating meaningful social connections is vital for sustaining optimal mental well-being. Engage in heartwarming interactions with friends, enveloped in laughter and exchanging life's moments. These connections are a robust pillar of support, instilling a renewed sense of belonging and reinforcing the intricate tapestry of human interdependence.

Nature Escapes: Immerse yourself in nature's untamed beauty, where every moment becomes an exhilarating adventure for the body and mind. Plan diverse nature excursions, from renting cabins for cozy retreats to exploring nearby state parks and historical sites. Consider staycations filled with hiking adventures or leisurely visits to botanical gardens. Engaging with the raw majesty of the natural world not only grounds us but also ignites our spirit, leaving us inspired and enveloped in profound tranquility.

Acts of Generosity: Engaging in acts of kindness extends beyond mere moments of goodwill; it's a transformative force reverberating through communities, leaving an indelible mark on both giver and recipient. Whether volunteering at local community centers, nursing homes, or libraries, mentoring individuals seeking guidance, or sharing insights as a guest speaker, each action contributes to a brighter, more connected world.

Moreover, donations to food banks and participation in programs like *Big Brothers Big Sisters of America* further amplify the impact, fostering a sense of purpose and joy that transcends individual interactions. As these acts ripple outward, they cultivate a culture of compassion, resilience, and holistic well-being, enriching lives and strengthening society's collective fabric.

Incorporating these essential wellness habits into your daily routine can help you feel more balanced and powerful in the face of life's challenges. So prioritize self-care, manage anxiety, quiet your mind, slow down, embrace nature, set realistic goals, eat mindfully, socialize, perform random acts of kindness, seek support, and remember to breathe! Your body, mind, and spirit will thank you for it.

"We can be sure that the greatest hope for maintaining equilibrium in the face of any situation rests within ourselves." —Francis J. Braceland

A Right Worthy Woman: A Novel by Ruth P. Watson

Based on the inspiring true story of Virginia's Black Wall Street and the indomitable Maggie Lena Walker, the daughter of a formerly enslaved woman who became the first Black woman to establish and preside over a bank in the United States.

Maggie Lena Walker was ambitious and unafraid. Her childhood in 19th-century Virginia helping her mother with her laundry service opened her eyes to the overwhelming discrepancy between the Black residents and her mother's affluent white clients.

She vowed to not only secure the same kind of home and finery for herself, but she would also help others in her community achieve the same.

With her single-minded determination, Maggie buckled down and went from schoolteacher to secretary-treasurer of the Independent Order of St. Luke, founder of a newspaper, a bank, and a department store where Black customers were treated with respect. With the help of influential friends like W.E.B. DuBois and Mary McLeod, she revolutionized Richmond in ways that are still felt today. Now, "with rich period detail and emotional impact" (Tracey Enerson Wood, author of The Engineer's Wife), her riveting full story is finally revealed in this stirring and intimate novel.

Raves and Reviews

"It is my distinct honor and pleasure to support this inspiring novel based on the life and times of Maggie Lena Walker, who was one of Zeta Phi Beta Sorority esteemed honorary members, inducted into our beloved organization in 1926."

– Dr. Valerie Hollingsworth Baker, 25th International Centennial President of Zeta Phi Beta Sorority Inc

"A character this richly complex and relentlessly determined deserves a place in the pantheon of great American entrepreneurs . . . Although our complicated racial history runs through this story, the author's skill as a novelist makes Walker's journey as enjoyable as it is inspiring."

– Pearl Cleage, award-winning playwright and bestselling author of What Looks Like Crazy on an Ordinary Day

Ruth P. Watson, an acclaimed author and versatile storyteller, has captivated readers with her compelling narratives across various genres. Her literary repertoire includes the bestsellers "*Blackberry Days of Summer*," "*An Elderberry Fall*," "*Cranberry Winter*," "*Strawberry Spring*," and "*A Right Worthy Woman*." These novels have been embraced by audiences worldwide.

The success of "*Blackberry Days of Summer*" inspired the creation of the musical stage play "Blackberry Daze," which premiered at Alexandria, Virginia's Metro Stage in September 2016. This adaptation received accolades, including a nomination for the prestigious Helen Hayes Award and a Suzi Bass Award nomination. Ruth's talent extends beyond prose into the realm of children's literature, with works such as "*Hard Lessons*" and "*Who Said a Girl Can't Be the President?*"

In addition to her literary achievements, Ruth is a multifaceted artist whose creative endeavors encompass freelance writing, documentary filmmaking, and stage productions. Her documentary work has been featured on the Public Broadcast Channel, notably with the documentary "*I've Paid My Dues, Now What?*" Ruth's dedication to inspiring both children and adults is evident in her commitment to education and community engagement. She serves as an adjunct professor and project manager and hosts the *Step Up and Pitch It Summit* in Atlanta, an event aimed at fostering understanding and participation in the city's burgeoning film and television industry.

Ruth's contributions to literature and the arts have been recognized through numerous accolades, including the Caversham Fellowship, an artist and writer's residency in KwaZulu-Natal, South Africa, where she published her first children's book in Zulu, titled "*Our Secret Bond*." Additionally, she was the first runner-up in the Frank Derby Literary Award.

A member of the Society of Children's Book Writers and Illustrators and a former Fulton County Arts Council appointee, Ruth is deeply engaged in fostering creativity and cultural enrichment within her community. She is also a proud member of Delta Sigma Theta Sorority Inc.

Ruth P. Watson resides in Atlanta, Georgia, where she resides with her family. She remains dedicated to her craft, seamlessly blending her passion for storytelling with her commitment to education and advocacy. Learn more at https://www.ruthpwatson.com

Double Lives (A Lexington, Alabama Novel) by Mary Monroe

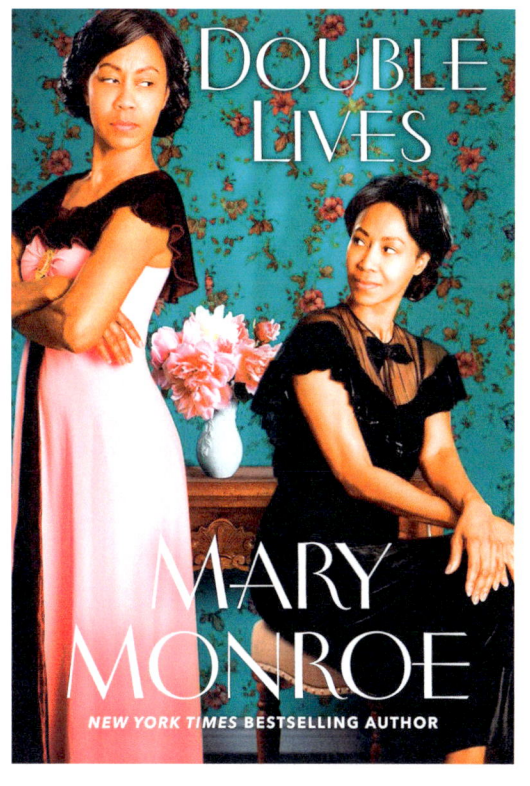

The latest shocking twist-filled novel in the award-winning New York Times bestselling author's Depression-era Alabama saga tells the riveting tale of identical twin sisters with a talent for switching lives and hiding their scandals—until one risk too many changes their lives forever. Reminiscent of Monroe's classic, captivating Mama Ruby series.

Since childhood, identical twins Leona and Fiona Dunbar have been getting in—and out—of trouble by pretending to be each other. Yet underneath, they couldn't be more different. Outspoken Leona lives to break rules, have a good time, and scandalize their respectable hometown of Lexington. Fiona is a seemingly-demure churchgoing girl who is the apple of her domineering, widowed mother Mavis's eye.

But together, the twins have fooled teachers, boyfriends, bosses, racist police—and most importantly, strait-laced Mavis. Even when Leona does jail time for Fiona, their unbreakable bond keeps them fiercely loyal. . . . So when Fiona feels stifled in her passionless marriage, and Leona is heartbroken over losing her one true love, it's perfect timing to change places once again . . .

Leona is shocked to discover she enjoys the security of being a wife and homebody. And the unexpected spark between her and Fiona's husband is giving her all kinds of deliciously sexy ideas. Meanwhile, Fiona enjoys being free, single, and reveling in the independence she's never had. And the more she indulges her secret, long-repressed wild child, the more Leona's ex-lover becomes one temptation she's having trouble resisting...

As the sisters' masquerade ignites desires and appetites they never expected, it also puts their most damning secrets on the line. Once the fallout rocks their small town, can Fiona and Leona's deep sisterhood shield them from total disaster and help them reconcile their mistakes? Or will the trust between them become a weapon that shatters their lives for good?

About the Author
Mary Monroe is the award-winning and New York Times bestselling author of more than 20 novels, with over one million books in print. The daughter of Alabama sharecroppers, she taught herself how to write before going on to become the first and only member of her family to finish high school. She lives in Oakland, California and can be found online at MaryMonroe.org.

Women of the Post by Joshunda Sanders

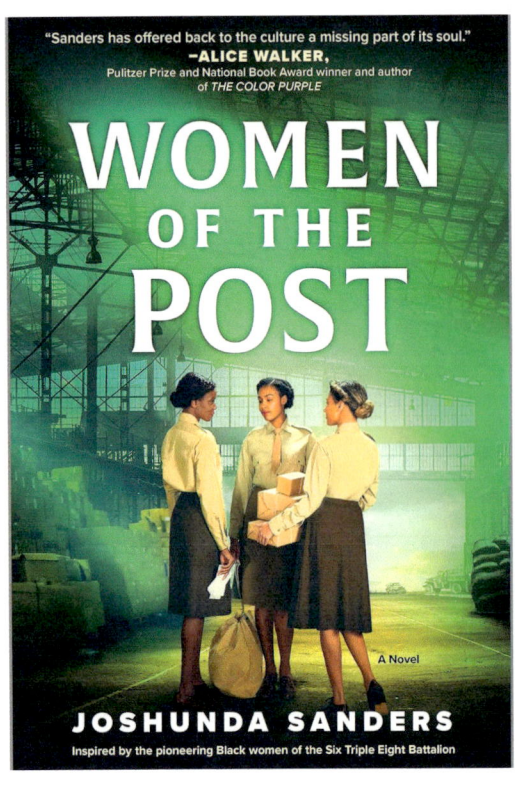

Women of the Post by Joshunda Sanders is an emotional story based on true events about the all-Black battalion of the Women's Army Corps, which found purpose, solidarity, and lifelong friendship in sorting over one million pieces of mail for the US Army.

"What a beautifully imagined and important narrative. Sanders' clear-eyed and powerful writing made this a hard one to stop reading!"
—Jacqueline Woodson, National Book Award-Winning Author

"This is a novel to cherish and share. And this is a history to sing about and affirm -- to proclaim."
— Honorée Fanonne Jeffers, New York Times Bestselling author of The Love Songs of W.E.B. Du Bois, an Oprah Book Club Novel

1944, New York City. Judy Washington is tired of having to work at the Bronx Slave Market, cleaning white women's houses for next to nothing. She dreams of a bigger life, but with her husband fighting overseas, it's up to her and her mother to earn enough for food and rent. When she's recruited to join the Women's Army Corps—offering a steady paycheck and the chance to see the world—Judy jumps at the opportunity.

During training, Judy becomes fast friends with the other women in her unit—Stacy, Bernadette and Mary Alyce—who all come from different cities and circumstances. Under Second Officer Charity Adams's leadership, they receive orders to sort over one million pieces of mail in England, becoming the only unit of Black women to serve overseas during WWII.

The women work diligently, knowing that they're reuniting soldiers with their loved ones through their letters. However, their work becomes personal when Mary Alyce discovers a backlogged letter addressed to Judy. Told through the alternating perspectives of Judy, Charity and Mary Alyce, Women of the Post is an unforgettable story of perseverance, female friendship and self-discovery.

Joshua Sanders is an Executive Communications leader/speechwriter. Her work has appeared in TIME Magazine, Poets & Writers, The New York Times, Oxford American and other publications. She has been the recipient of writing residencies or awards from the Martha's Vineyard Institute of Creative Writing, Lambda Literary, and the Key West Literary Seminars. In 2018, she was awarded the competitive Bronx Recognizes Its Own (BRIO) Award for excellence in fiction. She has taught writing and journalism at The School of the New York Times, Lehman College, the University of Texas Austin and The New School. She is the author of the children's books *I Can Write The World* and *A Place of Our Own*, the journalism textbook How Racism and Sexism Killed Traditional Media and the memoir *The Beautiful Darkness: A Handbook for Orphans*.

Let Us Descend: A Novel by Jesmyn Ward

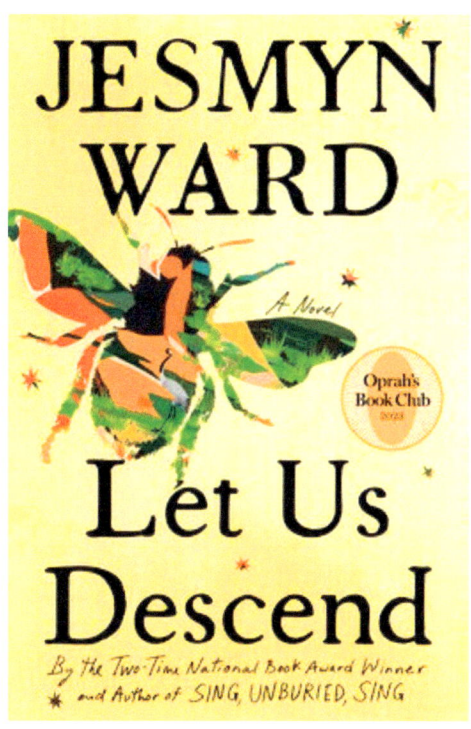

From "one of America's finest living writers" (San Francisco Chronicle) and "heir apparent to Toni Morrison" (LitHub)—comes a haunting masterpiece about an enslaved girl in the years before the Civil War that's destined to become a classic.

Let Us Descend describes a journey from the rice fields of the Carolinas to the slave markets of New Orleans and into the fearsome heart of a Louisiana sugar plantation.

A journey that is as beautifully rendered as it is heart wrenching, the novel is "the literary equivalent of an open wound from which poetry pours" (NPR).

Annis, sold south by the white enslaver who fathered her, is the reader's guide. As she struggles through the miles-long march, Annis turns inward, seeking comfort from memories of her mother and stories of her African warrior grandmother. Throughout, she opens herself to a world beyond this world, one teeming with spirits: of earth and water, of myth and history; spirits who nurture and give, and those who manipulate and take. While Annis leads readers through the descent, hers is ultimately a story of rebirth and reclamation.

From one of the most singularly brilliant and beloved writers of her generation, this "[s]earing and lyrical…raw, transcendent, and ultimately hopeful" (The Atlanta Journal-Constitution) novel inscribes Black American grief and joy into the very land—the rich but unforgiving forests, swamps, and rivers of the American South. Let Us Descend is Jesmyn Ward's most magnificent novel yet.

About Jesmyn Ward

Jesmyn Ward received her MFA from the University of Michigan and has received the MacArthur Genius Grant, a Stegner Fellowship, a John and Renee Grisham Writers Residency, the Strauss Living Prize, and the 2022 Library of Congress Prize for American Fiction. She is the historic winner—first woman and first Black American—of two National Book Awards for Fiction for Sing, Unburied, Sing (2017) and Salvage the Bones (2011). She is also the author of the novel Where the Line Bleeds and the memoir Men We Reaped, which was a finalist for the National Book Critics Circle Award and won the Chicago Tribune Heartland Prize and the Media for a Just Society Award. She is currently a professor of creative writing at Tulane University and lives in Mississippi.

Explore Books Written by Us for Us

Books We Love

BLACK WOMEN AUTHORS

SAVING RAINE BY MARIAN L. THOMAS

In the enchanting streets of Paris, Raine Reynolds sought refuge from a heartache that seemed impossible to escape. But even as she wandered thousands of miles from her past, the pain clung to her like a relentless shadow.

Now, as the senior VP of a thriving ad agency, Raine is forced to return to a city brimming with memories she'd rather forget. Atlanta is where every street corner whispers of a life she once had.

But as life would have it, an old friend resurfaces, offering a glimmer of healing in the midst of her turmoil. Can she summon the courage to trust and love once more, to embark on a journey of resilience and redemption?

Join Raine on an inspiring journey through the turbulent waters of her past as she battles adversity, loss, and the quest for redemption. "Saving Raine" is a tale of unwavering resilience and the redemptive power of love.

It's a story that reminds us all that even in the darkest of times, hope can be found, and the human spirit can rise above any challenge.

Excerpt: Saving Raine by Marian L. Thomas

There comes a moment in life when you find yourself standing at a fork in the road, undecided, unsure, knowing you have to make a decision. This way, or that? The route to the left offers a chance of fleeing from life so fast you can't catch your breath, escaping to an easier place where you can hide away for a while. On your right, you're standing in the middle of the road, stripped bare, somehow devoid of feeling, and yet ensnared in the worst possible agony, screaming until the tears come cascading down your face.

As my house keys nestle in my sweaty palm, fingers curled way too tight around them, poised outside our five-bedroomed home, I know which road I'm on. In truth, the moment my swollen eyes shot open this morning, and my head lifted from a tear-soaked pillow, it was apparent. However, the fact that I slipped on a pair of dark blue jeans that I haven't worn since the day James and I met and a white satin blouse that James loved but I hated because it had a shine to it confirms that my feet have more than drifted to the right.

But now, as I stand here staring at our fiery red front door, this wretched satin blouse is clinging to my body like Saran Wrap, I can't determine if it's clinging because this afternoon sun in September has my skin as hot as a cup of freshly made McDonald's coffee or because my body is clinging to a love that has taken up every inch of my heart for the last fifteen years. Perhaps, it's a little bit of both. Right now, all I can think about is how I'd give anything for a breeze or something to carry me from here. I pray for anything, anything at all, to rescue me.

In the past, the heady aroma of fall flowers would have filled my lungs sufficiently to alleviate the anxiety occupying this space, but today, not so. Today, even the violas and pansies that break into bud and bloom around this time of the year seem vacant of any scent, and the more I stand here, the more my mind longs for something to whisk me up into the clouds where I can just float away and pretend like I don't have a care in the world or a broken heart. At this moment, I'd give anything to be able to look down at my life instead of standing in front of what it used to be. Trying to breathe.

If anyone were to walk by right now, they would say that I was well put together, only witnessing what's on the surface of my outer appearance, the inner masked so well. They wouldn't look hard enough to see what was brewing inside. And what if they did? What if they took just a second to step back? Well, they would see the very sinews and veins of me, no outer skin, no protection, just stark vulnerability, and lungs worn out from screaming. And if those same onlookers took another second to peer even closer, then, they would see a mad stream of tears only a few split seconds away from breaking free and rushing down the sides of my face.

I take a slow and deliberate deep breath as I slip my house key into the door's lock. It moves with familiarity, bringing back a host of memories better left subdued. The heavy door clicks open, my hand rests on the solid brass handle that James and I had fought over.

"Too old fashioned," he'd said. "The sort of handle an old person would have." That all changed once Damon, our handyman, installed it. "Great choice," James then said. "Really suits the door and frame, gives a kind of luxurious feel." In the end, it became his idea.

How can it be that in everyday life when everything's normal, you don't think twice about the simple stuff like opening a door, or picking out a door handle, until those simple things remind you that another woman placed her hands on them too, acting as if they belonged to her. As if my James, too, was hers to touch and to kiss and to keep. The worst part of all of this is that I can't ask James the one question that continues to burn in my heart. *Why?*

(Continued...)

Copyright 2024 All rights reserved. Book excerpt reprinted by permission of the author, Marian L. Thomas.

Soignée Sisterhood Conversation - Marian L. Thomas

Marian L. Thomas is the award-winning author of The Caged Butterfly and Saving Raine–winners of the USA Best Book Awards for African-American Fiction. With a passion for creating stories that deeply resonate with women, Marian invites readers on a transformative journey through her latest work, "Saving Raine." This captivating novel delves into the unyielding human spirit, leaving readers inspired and empowered. Through her writing, Marian sheds light on themes of resilience, love, and hope, providing a powerful perspective that uplifts and motivates women.

SLM: Marian, "Saving Raine" is a deeply emotional and compelling story. Can you tell us what inspired you to write a novel with such intricate themes of loss, betrayal, and redemption?
Marian L. Thomas: Thank you for having me! "Saving Raine" was born out of a fascination with the human spirit and its capacity to endure even the most painful circumstances. I wanted to explore the heart's resilience when faced with betrayal and tragedy and the enduring power of love to heal wounds. The story was also inspired by the idea that sometimes, we run from our problems, but ultimately, we find the strength to confront them head-on.

SLM: The book's protagonist, Raine Reynolds, experiences profound loss and betrayal throughout the story. Can you share how Raine's journey reflects themes of resilience and redemption?
Marian L. Thomas: Absolutely. Raine's journey is a testament to the human spirit's ability to rise above adversity. She faces unimaginable loss, from the tragic accident that took her child and father to the heart-wrenching betrayal of her husband's infidelity. Despite these hardships, Raine discovers her own inner strength and resilience. It's a journey of self-discovery and healing, ultimately leading to redemption through forgiveness and love.

SLM: Can you tell us more about Donovan Carter, a pivotal figure in Raine's life, and how their relationship evolves throughout the story?
Marian L. Thomas: Donovan Carter is a character who carries his own burdens from the past. He's a friend from Raine's past and a symbol of hope and redemption. As Raine and Donovan reconnect after years apart, their relationship evolves from a chance encounter to a deep and meaningful connection. Donovan becomes a source of support and understanding for Raine, helping her navigate her challenges.

SLM: Therapy plays a significant role in the story, with Raine and Detective Tracy Thompson benefiting. Can you speak to the importance of seeking help when dealing with trauma and grief?
Marian L. Thomas: Therapy is a central theme in "Saving Raine" because it highlights the importance of seeking help and support when dealing with trauma and grief. It's a reminder that we don't have to face our pain alone and that there is strength in vulnerability. Therapy provides Raine and Tracy with the tools to heal and move forward, showing that it's okay to ask for help when we need it.

Soignée Sisterhood Conversation - Marian L. Thomas

SLM: The book also explores the theme of forgiveness. Can you elaborate on how forgiveness plays a role in Raine's journey toward healing and redemption?

Marian L. Thomas: Forgiveness is a powerful theme in the story. Raine is faced with the challenge of forgiving not only her husband but also herself for her perceived shortcomings. Through forgiveness, she finds the strength to let go of her pain and anger, ultimately paving the way for healing and redemption. It's a reminder that forgiveness is a gift we give ourselves, allowing us to move forward and find peace.

SLM: The novel takes readers on a journey from Paris to Atlanta and back. How do these different settings contribute to the overall narrative?

Marian L. Thomas: The settings in "Saving Raine" are more than just locations; they are symbolic of Raine's emotional journey. Paris represents her escape from her past, while Atlanta is a place of memories and challenges. Each setting reflects a different phase of her life and the evolving emotions she experiences. They serve as a backdrop for her transformation and growth.

SLM: Can you tell us about the role of secondary characters like Jasmine and Brianna in Raine's life and how they influence her path to healing?

Marian L. Thomas: Jasmine and Brianna are essential to Raine's journey. Jasmine, Raine's friend, reveals painful truths about Raine's past and helps her confront her husband's betrayal. Brianna, on the other hand, represents new beginnings and offers Raine companionship and support when she needs it most. These secondary characters provide different perspectives and sources of strength in Raine's life.

SLM: Can you share what readers can expect from the ending of "Saving Raine"?

Marian L. Thomas: The ending of "Saving Raine" is a culmination of Raine's journey of resilience and redemption. It's a conclusion that offers hope, healing, and the promise of a new beginning. Readers can expect closure for Raine and the other characters, as well as a sense of fulfillment that mirrors their own emotional journey throughout the novel.

SLM: Lastly, what message or takeaway do you hope readers will find in "Saving Raine"?

Marian L. Thomas: At its core, "Saving Raine" is a story of hope and the indomitable human spirit. I hope readers will take away the message that no matter how challenging life may become, there is always a path to healing, redemption, and love. It's a reminder that we can find strength in our vulnerabilities and that forgiveness can lead to the most profound transformations in our lives.

Connect with Marian L. Thomas

Website: https://marianlthomas.com
X/Twitter: https://twitter.com/marianlthomas01
Instagram: https://www.instagram.com/marianlthomas09
Facebook: https://www.facebook.com/marianlthomasbooks

Soignée Sisterhood Spotlight
Janet Autherine, Author. Speaker. Mentor

"Island Mindfulness: How to Use the Transformational Power of Mindfulness to Create an Abundant Life is my life story. It is the book that I wished for my younger self. I hope it continues to empower overwhelmed women to create a balanced, peaceful, highly successful, and abundant life.

Growing into Greatness is a series of books and a community of mentors that teach teens, young adults, and lifelong learners how to triumph over limiting beliefs, power through obstacles, and confidently grow into their own definition of greatness.

Founder of the Growing into Greatness Mentorship Community, Janet teaches young adults how to triumph over limiting beliefs and confidently grow into their own definition of greatness by mastering the 10 Tenets of Greatness.

Janet immigrated from Jamaica as a teenager and knows what it is like to overcome the odds and accomplish one's dreams. She graduated from Boston College Law School and has served in the legal community for over 25 years. She is the author of five books focused on empowering women and children.

Through her mentorship initiatives, Growing into Greatness and Women Leaving Footprints, she creates a bridge of knowledge that enables young adults to receive the mentorship that she lacked during her early career.

Janet is a mom to three wonderful boys, a runner, and an inspirational writer. She is active in several bar associations, Mediators Beyond Borders, and the Rotary Club.

Author Page: https://www.janetautherine.com
Amazon: https://www.amazon.com/Janet-Autherine/e/B00KXINZJM

Unleash Your Inner Poet
A Self-Guided Masterclass in Writing Poetry Books

"Poetry is emotion that has been set free."

Janet Autherine is an accomplished author and poet. She is the author of the poetry books *Wild Heart, Peaceful Soul*, and the *Heart and Soul of Black Women*. She has a heart for mentoring aspiring poets and writers. Janet is the author of the self-guided course, *Unleash Your Inner Poet - A Masterclass* that will supercharge your writing and propel you from idea to book in as little as 60 days.

This masterclass empowers aspiring poets to transform emotions and life experiences into a compelling poetry book. Through insightful lessons and practical exercises, students will discover their unique voice & master the art of poetry writing.

If you have been eager to birth a poetry book, Janet's unique blend of passion, expertise, and positivity will inspire and empower you to reach new heights in your writing journey. Here's a glimpse into the path:

Chapter 1: "Need Inspiration? We Have You Covered" - Discover endless sources of inspiration.

Chapter 2: "Clear the Mental Blocks to Writing" - Break down the barriers to your creativity.

Chapter 3: "Crafting Your Poetic Voice" - Find and refine your unique poetic expression.

Chapter 4: "Mastering the Art of Imagery" - Paint vivid pictures with your words.

Chapter 5: "Exploring Emotions Through Poetry" - Dive deep into your feelings and bring them to life.

Chapter 6: "Your Highly Effective Daily Writing Routine" - Develop a writing practice that fuels your creativity.

Chapter 7: "Self-Publishing Your Poetry Book" - Navigate the journey to publishing with confidence.

Unleash Your Inner Poet
A Self-Guided Masterclass in Writing Poetry Books

This transformative experience includes a comprehensive workbook and a 45-day writing calendar designed to support and inspire your poetic journey.

Janet Autherine believes that the art of poetry is transformative. Poetry gives you the freedom to be one with yourself in a discipline where every part of your being is embraced. Poetry gives your emotions room to travel to a destination that is a safe space without walls or boundaries and with complete freedom of expression. Join her on the journey.

Unlock your creative potential by enrolling in the Unleash Your Inner Poet Masterclass. Scan the QR code or visit https://bit.ly/3xcbs4O

Love, Struggle and Resilience

Lest you get weary
Lest you lose faith and forget your magnificence
when faced with that other ism that resides
at the intersection of race and gender

Rest your soul on the shoulders of your band of sisters
Black woman - feminist - womanist - fighter

Holding up two heavy banners for freedom and
passing them from generation to generation
because there is no cure for racism and sexism

Write the name of each soldier in the journal
of every Black girl who needs to go into the world
armed with the fighting spirit of our heroes

Shirley Chisholm
Dorothy Height
Frances Ellen Watkins Harper
Ida B. Wells
Angela Davis
Audre Lorde
Pauli Murray
Mary Church Terrell
Sojourner Truth

and the many other brave women
who gave meaning to the words
— PROUD and Black and
WOMAN

The Heart and Soul of Black Women: Poems of Love, Struggle and Resilience by Janet Autherine

The Heart and Soul of Black Women celebrates Black women's beauty, vulnerability, and humanity. It is the healing, uplifting, and heartbreaking stories of all aspects of our human journey through the art of poetry.

Inside, you will find poems addressing powerful issues, such as Mothers of Black Boys, Black Love, Self-Worth, Strong Sisters Unite, Raising Special Needs Children, Addiction and Abuse, Single Motherhood, Healthy Dating, and Standing for Justice and Equality in the Face of Racism.

"My sisters, we are precious and vulnerable and resilient and powerful. We are the dream of our ancestors. We deserve to hold our heads high, walk in strength, cry openly, and get angry without being labeled an angry Black woman. We are human. Our hearts break and mend.

We don't always bounce back from adversity as fast as expected; we sometimes need therapy and an extra dose of love. As a matter of fact, we need deep and abiding love. I hope that when you read these poems, you see all the beauty and complexity that is inside. I hope that you see your majesty, and the world sees your humanity."
– Janet Autherine

SEE US

Take 2 steps closer
Extend your hand
Touch our hearts
Feel our spirits
We are fearful,
yet we are strong

SEE US

We are vulnerable,
yet we are resilient
Our hearts break easily,
yet we love deeply
We are human
See our humanity
See us

Wild Heart, Peaceful Soul: Poems & Inspiration to Live and Love Harmoniously by J. Autherine

Janet Autherine's inaugural collection of poems and inspiration is a love offering to women who lead with their hearts, love deeply, and sometimes fall hard.

Wild Heart, Peaceful Soul is a deep, gritty, raw look at the thrill of loving unconditionally and the mental and physical toll it takes when peace and harmony are lost in the process. The author draws inspiration from her own journey spanning 30 years and also dives deeply into the vulnerable hearts of women globally, including her experience growing up in Jamaica.

She captures the pain and struggle of women who love deeply and pour into others without first filling their own jars. A recurring theme is reclaiming your heart in order to live and love harmoniously.

Chapter one, *Wild Heart*, takes the reader on a journey of self-discovery — being an empath in a sometimes harsh world, feeling broken after losing love, not feeling good enough to be loved, facing rejection and abandonment, and navigating life with a heart that just wants to love unconditionally.

The second chapter, *Peaceful Soul*, is an empowering meditation on the peace that comes with reclaiming your heart — finding strength in the love and support of sister friends, practicing self-love while responsibly loving others, and finding joy in loving those who are worthy of our love.

Wild Heart, Peaceful Soul is a patchwork of vulnerability, truth, and empowerment for everyone who loves deeply.

No Reservations: A Novel of Friendship by Sheryl Lister

Get ready for the ultimate girls' trip as women's fiction author Sheryl Lister celebrates the power of friendship and living a life with no reservations.

True friendship never ends.

Best friends forever. That's the vow Joy, Diane, Rochelle and Yvette made when they were children, and even in their mid-thirties, the friends have always been there for each other—through the highs and lows of life and love. Until forever comes up against a terminal cancer diagnosis. Nothing could have prepared them for what life would look like when four became three.

But Yvette was prepared.

Her final gift to her girls is an all-expenses-paid trip to Jamaica like they had always talked about but kept putting off as life got in the way.

The Jamaican getaway can't come soon enough as the remaining friends deal with their grief, dashed hopes, and unexpected relationship drama. Sick of putting her dreams to open a spa on hold, not to mention her husband's lack of support, Joy decides she's moving forward with her new business—with or without him. The thunderous ticking of Diane's biological clock has her wondering if her desire to have a baby will ever come true, and her husband's bizarre behavior has her questioning if he's still on board. And after witnessing her friends' imploding relationships, single mother Rochelle is content to do life on her own, but her heart doesn't seem to get the memo when a new man unexpectedly enters the picture.

Guided by Yvette's spirit, the friends must lean on each other now more than ever before as they learn to navigate their new normal, take unexpected risks and live life with no reservations.

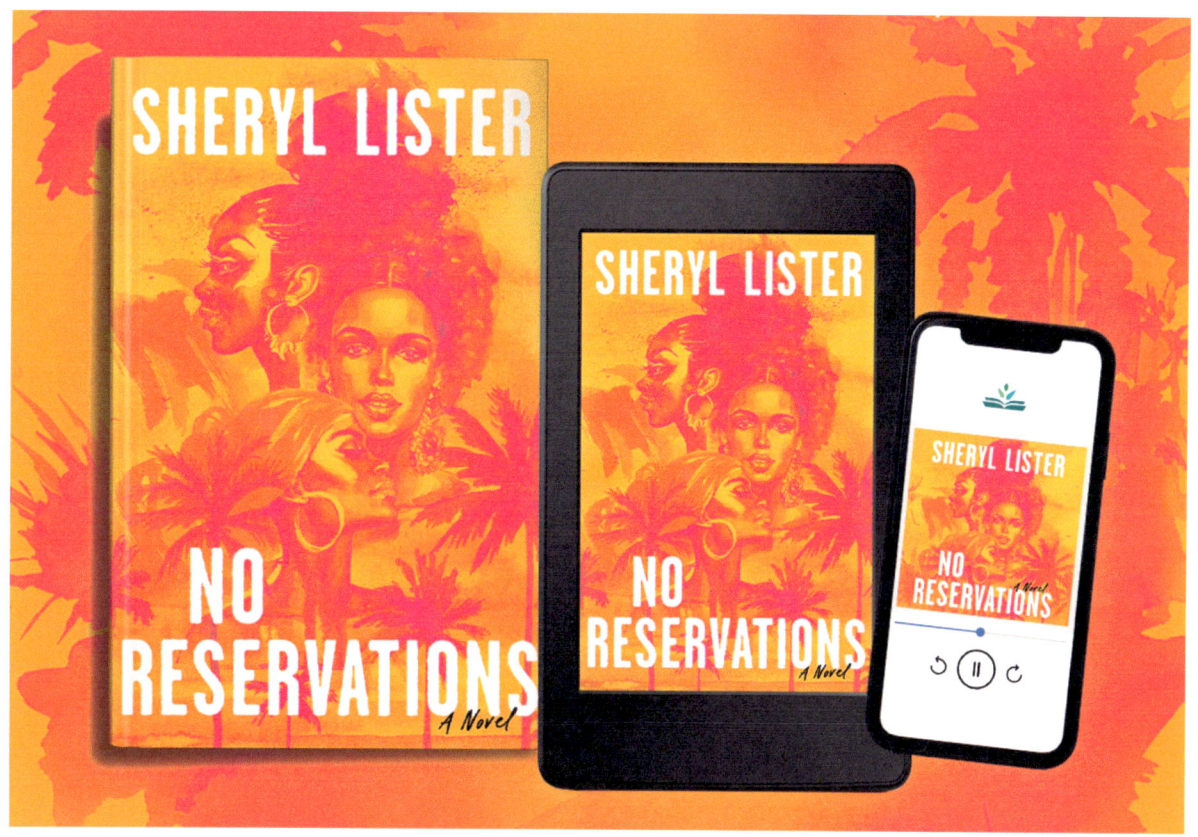

No Reservations: A Novel of Friendship by Sheryl Lister

"Joy, your mama named you right because you've been that and more to me. You've sacrificed your dreams long enough, sis. It's time for you to start that business because every woman needs a place of respite."

Joy laughed through her tears and gave Yvette's hand a gentle squeeze. "I know, and I promise."

Yvette shifted her gaze to her second friend. "Diane, you've been the best godmother to Ebony and Ian— all three of you have— and I know you'll be an even better mother. Jeff will come around, just keep working on him."

Diane's pained gaze met Yvette's. "I'm working on him. One way or another," she added with a wry smile.

"Rochelle," Yvette started.

Before she could continue, Rochelle lifted a hand. "I already know what you're going to say."

Joy laughed. "Probably the same thing we've all been saying."

Yvette chuckled, then moaned in pain. "Don't make me laugh. Chelle, girl, I know your sorry ex is enough to make a woman stay single for the rest of this life and the next, but you're a beautiful woman, and you can't do that. Warren is a good man, and he really likes you."

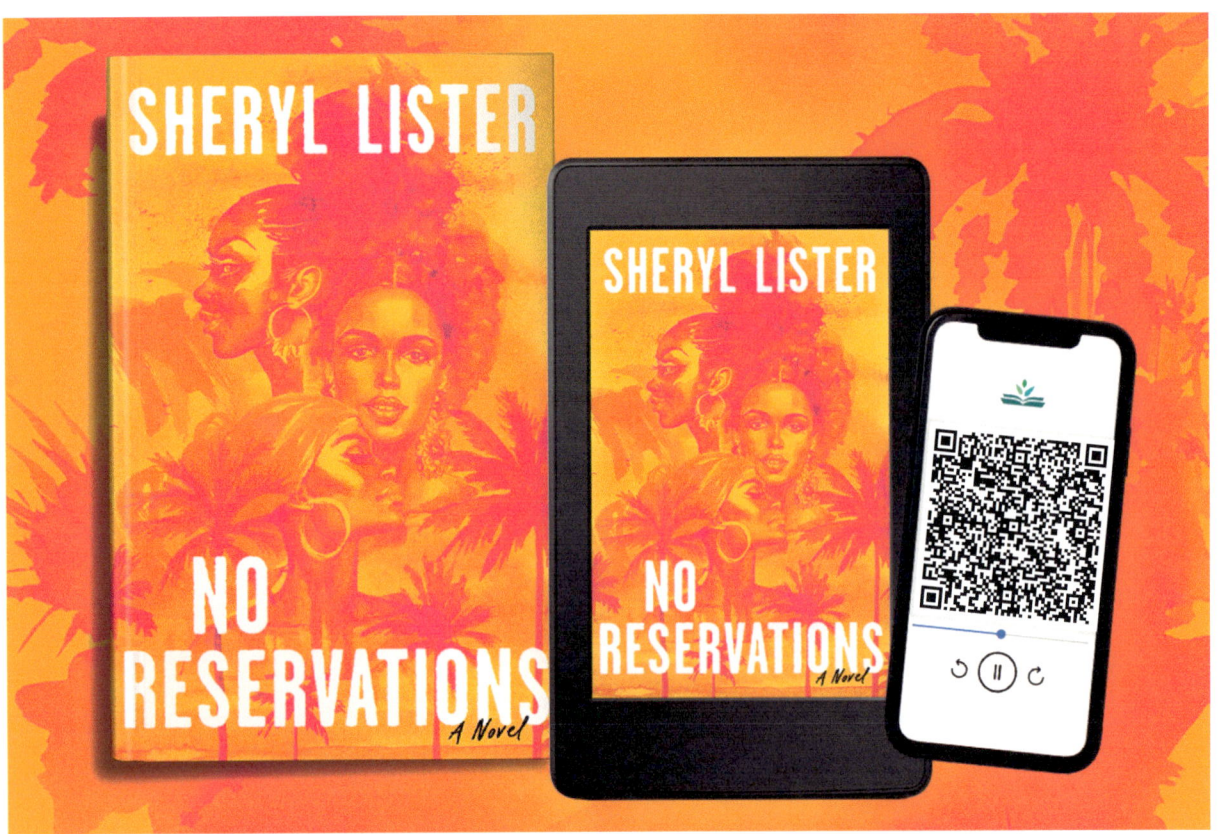

No Reservations: A Novel of Friendship by Sheryl Lister

Rochelle raised an eyebrow. "How do you know?"

"I asked. What did you think? Let him in, sis. He can love you like you deserve to be loved." She grasped Rochelle's hand.

"I'll see." Yvette gave her a look. "Hey, it's the best I can do." "

Joy and Di, make sure she doesn't mess it up."

"We will," they chorused.

"Watch out for Joe and my babies, okay? And if he finds somebody else, be nice to her." She smiled at Joe. "Well, unless she's a gold- digging heifer. Oh, one more thing. We never got around to taking that trip back to Jamaica. Don't put it off any longer. Make those reservations, and take that trip."

(Continued...)

Copyright 2024 All rights reserved. Book excerpt reprinted with permission from the author. Purchase your copy of No Reservations on Amazon: https://amzn.to/3zAP2Z0

About Sheryl Lister
Sheryl Lister is an award-winning author who writes sweet, sensual contemporary romance, romantic suspense and women's fiction. Her novels feature multi-faceted, intelligent, strong and slightly flawed heroes and heroines. Away from writing, she spends her time whipping up delicious meals and desserts to satisfy her inner foodie.

Janice Trachtman

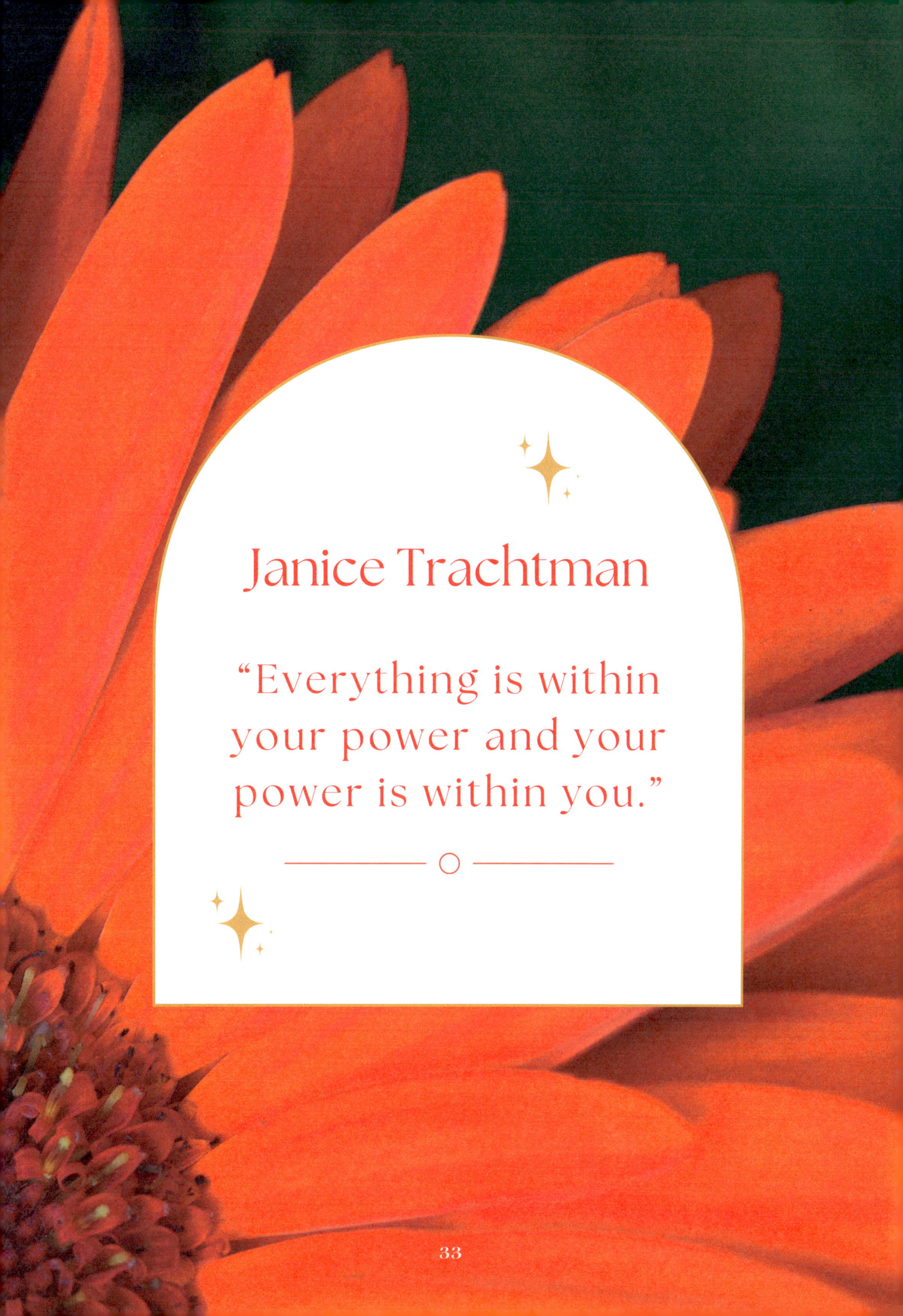

"Everything is within your power and your power is within you."

PREYING TIME TRILOGY
BY TRACIE LOVELESS HILL

PREYING TIME by Tracie Loveless Hill

The Reverend Randall C. Harris, pastor of a large and prominent church, seems to have it all. He is handsome, charismatic, influential, and well-loved by his congregation and beautiful wife. Reverend Harris is deeply spiritual. He's involved in the community and dedicated to his church members—especially females.

"Yes, I am a man of God, but first and foremost, I am a man." These words are Reverend Harris's rationale for his actions that might not align with Christian ethics. He truly believes he's entitled to pursue the delights of the flesh as long as he fulfills the duties of his ministry, but Reverend Harris will find that there are terrible consequences to pay when what should be praying time becomes preying time.

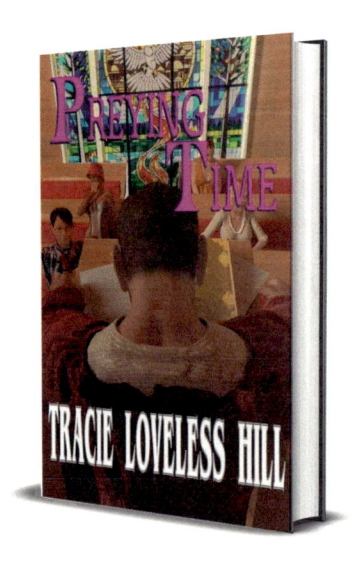

STILL PREYING by Tracie Loveless Hill

After being shot and nearly killed, Rev. Randall Harris is a changed man. He has become a good husband and a dedicated Pastor, and he's turned his life over to the Lord. But his former right-hand man, Deacon Samuel Wise, seems poised to take over where Rev. Harris left off. Deacon Wise wants the old Rev. Harris back—the scoundrel who once ran the streets with him and preyed on the women of the congregation. Deacon Wise is on his own, though, and continues to lead a secret life built on lies, cheating—and, eventually, theft. When Unity Missionary Baptist Church receives a hefty inheritance from one of its beloved members, Deacon Wise schemes to see if he can get his hands on some of it—but he's treading on dangerous ground without his old 'partner in crime' to cover for him. When violence brings everything to a head, the good Deacon could lose all he's worked for and risk the safety of those he cares about—and all because he is…Still Preying!

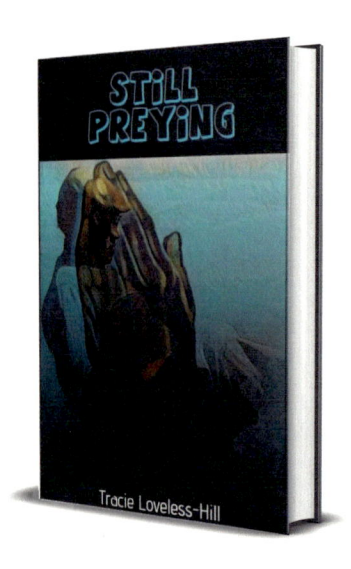

PREYING HARD TIME by Tracie Loveless Hill

Like a pebble dropped into water, actions have a ripple effect and touch everyone around. In a drug deal gone wrong, Montel had once shot the Reverend Randall C. Harris, leaving a bullet in his head. Confined to a wheelchair after being shot in the back, Montel suffers a similar fate. This is made worse by the fact that he is behind bars, serving a lengthy prison sentence. With time stretched out before him, Montel has every opportunity to think about what landed him in prison and how he may redeem himself once he's served his sentence—if he can make it out alive. With trouble so easy to find in prison, how will he avoid pitfalls that could turn his bid into a life sentence? With folks who believe in him, against the odds, Montel finds a 'guardian angel,' a renewed outlook, and forgiveness while he is…Preying Hard Time.

Soignée Sisterhood Conversation
Tracie Loveless Hill

Tracie Loveless-Hill, born and raised in Waterloo, Iowa, has spent 35 years married to her soulmate, Cedric. They share the joys of parenthood with their two wonderful children, Taneya and Cedric II.

Her educational journey began at Hawkeye Community College, where she earned associate degrees in criminology and general studies. She then continued her studies at Rust College in Holly Springs, Mississippi, an esteemed Historically Black College and University (HBCU). Tracie's professional background is rich with experience, having served as a Communications Specialist at U.S. West before retiring.

However, her commitment to her community extends far beyond the workplace. Raised in the nurturing embrace of Mount Carmel Missionary Baptist Church, where she accepted Christ at a tender age, Tracie's passion for community involvement stems from her upbringing under the guidance of her beloved Grandmother, C.M. Powell-Ambrose.

Recognized as a dedicated community activist, Tracie actively engages in initiatives aimed at enhancing the well-being of her community and its residents. Yet, amidst her various roles and responsibilities, Tracie finds solace and joy in simple pleasures—whether it's immersing herself in the pages of a captivating novel, being uplifted by the melodies of traditional gospel music, or cherishing quality time with her cherished family, who remain her greatest source of happiness and fulfillment.

SLM: Thank you for joining us today, Tracie Loveless-Hill. We're excited to learn more about your inspiring journey and the purpose that drives you. To start off, please tell us a bit about the influence your grandmothers had on shaping your purpose in life.
Tracie Loveless-Hill: Absolutely! My grandmothers were truly remarkable individuals who instilled in me the values of compassion, resilience, and community. They taught me that regardless of our circumstances or the challenges we face, we have a responsibility to care for one another and make a positive impact in the world. Their unwavering love and selflessness inspire me constantly.

SLM: That's incredibly touching. It's clear that their influence runs deep in your life. Can you elaborate on how their teachings led you to your current endeavors, such as creating a library/media center and a child care center in your community?
Tracie Loveless-Hill: Certainly. Their teachings laid the foundation for my commitment to serving others and fostering community connections. I wanted to create spaces where people of all ages could come together to learn, grow, and support one another. The library/media center provides access to resources and technology that empower individuals to expand their knowledge and skills. Similarly, the Child Care Center offers a safe and nurturing environment for children, allowing parents to pursue their own goals while knowing their children are well-cared for.

SLM: It's wonderful to hear about the tangible ways in which you're making a difference in your community. Can you tell us more about the causes you're passionate about supporting?
Tracie Loveless-Hill: Absolutely! In addition to the library and Child Care Center, I'm deeply committed to several causes that are close to my heart.

Soignée Sisterhood Conversation
Tracie Loveless Hill

I'm passionate about supporting veterans, addressing homelessness, advocating for rescued animals, and combating food insecurity. These are issues that affect countless individuals and families, and it's our collective responsibility to take action and create positive change.

SLM: Your dedication to such diverse causes is truly commendable. How do you envision your work bringing people together and fostering unity within your community?
Tracie Loveless-Hill: I believe that by providing spaces for reading, conversation, and direct community action, we can bridge divides and build connections among people from all walks of life. Whether it's through discussing a book at the library, volunteering at a local shelter, or organizing a food drive, these shared experiences can break down barriers and unite us in our common humanity. My hope is that through our collective efforts, we can create a more compassionate and inclusive community where everyone feels valued and supported.

SLM: That's a powerful vision for the future. Let's shift gears a bit and talk about your latest literary work, the *Preying Time Trilogy*. Can you tell us about the inspiration behind this series?
Tracie Loveless-Hill: The *Preying Time Trilogy* delves into the complexities of faith, morality, and the human experience. It explores the consequences of Reverend Randall C. Harris's actions when what should be praying time becomes preying time.

SLM: The premise of the first book sounds intriguing and thought-provoking. How do the subsequent books in the trilogy continue this narrative?
Tracie Loveless-Hill: In "Still Preying," readers follow the aftermath of Reverend Harris's transformation and the challenges he faces as he strives to live a changed life. Meanwhile, Deacon Samuel Wise, a former associate, continues to lead a secret life of deceit and betrayal.

The final installment, "Preying Hard Time," shifts focus to Montel, a character seeking redemption while navigating the challenges of prison life.

SLM: The trilogy sounds like a gripping journey through complex moral terrain. How do you hope readers will resonate with your books?
Tracie Loveless-Hill: My hope is that the *Preying Time Trilogy* will spark meaningful conversations about faith and the consequences of our actions. I want readers to be challenged to confront difficult truths and consider how we grapple with questions of forgiveness, redemption, and the search for meaning in the face of adversity.

SLM: Thank you, Tracie Loveless-Hill, for sharing your compelling trilogy. We wish you continued success in your literary endeavors and community service efforts.
Tracie Loveless-Hill: Thank you for having me. It's been a pleasure to discuss my work and the issues that matter to me.

Website: www.tracielovelesshill.com
Facebook: www.facebook.com/authoresstracie
Find her books on Amazon: https://amzn.to/49iMgHt

Empowerment

"You are on the eve of a complete victory. You can't go wrong. The world is behind you."
– Josephine Baker

A Passionate Mind in Relentless Pursuit
The Vision of Mary McLeod Bethune by Noliwe Rooks

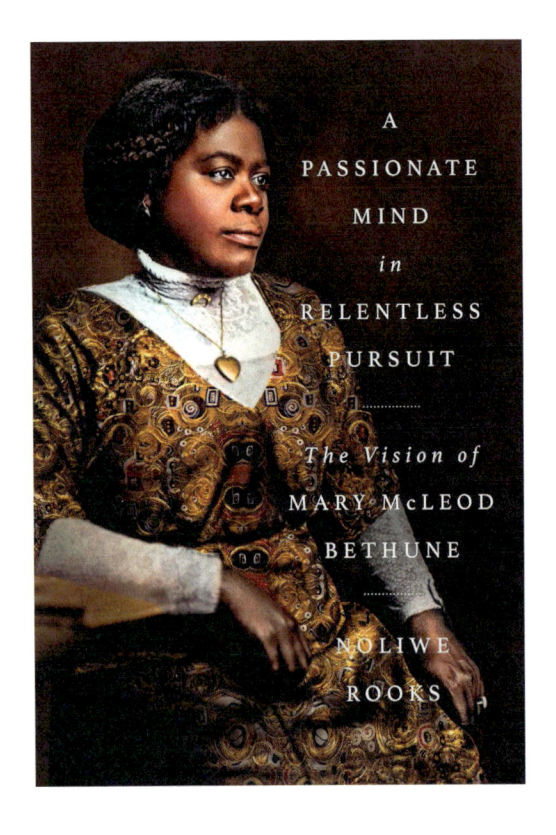

An intimate and searching account of the life and legacy of one of America's towering educators, a woman who dared to center the progress of Black women and girls in the larger struggle for political and social liberation

When Mary McLeod Bethune died, newspaper tributes said the same thing: she should be on the Mount Rushmore of Black American achievement. Indeed, Dr. Mary McLeod Bethune is the first African American represented in the National Statuary Hall Collection.

Mary McLeod Bethune became the first Black statue ever erected on federal lands and yet for most, she remains a marble figure from the dim past.

Now, seventy years later, Noliwe Rooks turns Bethune from stone to flesh, showing her to be a visionary leader with lessons to still teach us as we continue our journey toward a freer and more just nation. Any serious effort to understand how the Black civil rights generation found role models, vision, and inspiration during their midcentury struggle for political power must place Bethune at its heart. Her success was unlikely: the fifteenth of seventeen children and the firstborn into freedom, Bethune survived brutal poverty and caste subordination to become the first in her family to learn how to read and to attend college.

She gave that same gift to others when in 1904, at age twenty-nine, Bethune welcomed her first class of five girls to the Daytona, Florida, school she had founded and which would become the university that bears her name to this day. Bethune saw education as an essential dimension of the larger struggle for freedom, vitally connected to the vote and to economic self-sufficiency, and she enlisted Eleanor Roosevelt, Harry Truman, Franklin D. Roosevelt, and many other powerful leaders in her cause.

The story of how Bethune succeeded in a state with some of the highest lynching rates in the country is, in Rooks's hands, a moving and astonishing example of the power of a mind and a vision that had few equals. Now, when the stakes of the long struggle for full Black equality in this country are particularly evident—and centered on the state of Florida—it is a gift to have this brilliant and lyrical reckoning with Bethune's journey from one of our own great educators and scholars of that same struggle.

A Passionate Mind in Relentless Pursuit
The Vision of Mary McLeod Bethune by Noliwe Rooks

Rooks grew up in Florida, in Bethune's shadow: her grandmother trained to be a teacher at Bethune-Cookman University, and her family vacationed at the all-Black beach that Bethune helped found in one of her many community empowerment projects.

Book Review

"In reflecting on Mary McLeod Bethune's life and on her own, Noliwe Rooks offers a tribute to an inspiring leader and a meditation on race and history."
—**Drew Faust, Arthur Kingsley Porter University Research Professor, Harvard University**

About the Author

An interdisciplinary scholar, Noliwe Rooks is the L. Herbert Ballou University Professor of Africana Studies, and the chair of Africana Studies at Brown University. Her work explores how race and gender both impact and are impacted by popular culture, social history and political life in the United States. She works on the cultural and racial implications of beauty, fashion and adornment; race, capitalism and education, and the urban politics of food and cannabis production.

The author of five books, including *A Passionate Mind in Relentless Pursuit: The Vision of Mary McLeod Bethune*, is also the author of numerous articles, essays and Op-Ed's, Rooks has received research funding from the Ford Foundation, the Mellon Foundation and the Woodrow Wilson School among others.

She lectures frequently at colleges and universities around the country and is a regular contributor to popular outlets such as The New York Times, The Washington Post, The Chronicle of Higher Education, Time Magazine and NPR.

Rooks' book, in which she coined the term "segrenomics," *Cutting School: Privatization, Segregation, and the End of Public Education* won an award from the Hurston/Wright Foundation. Her current book project explores how the implementation of integration/desegregation strategies impacted Black children and communities. It is tentatively titled, *Integration, An American Dream*, and explores four generations of her family history with integration and educational experimentation.

Emancipation's Daughters: Reimagining Black Femininity and the National Body by Riché Richardson

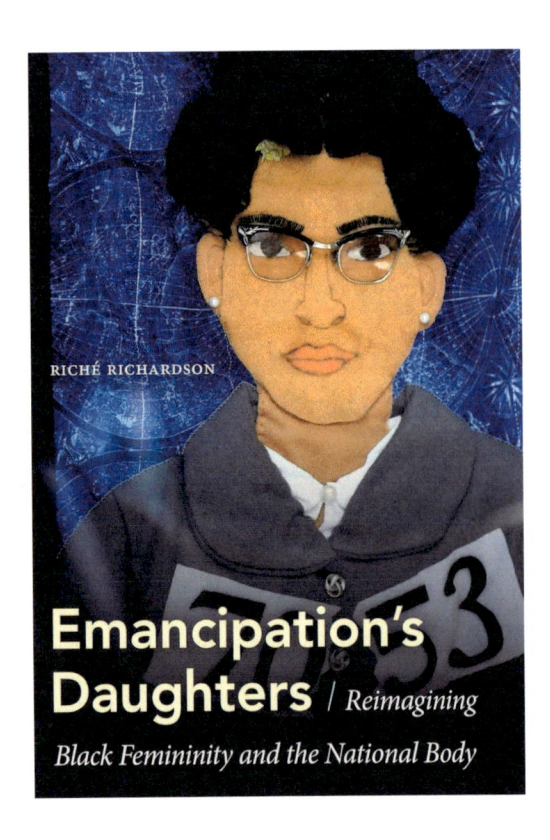

In *Emancipation's Daughters*, Riché Richardson examines iconic black women leaders who have contested racial stereotypes and constructed new national narratives of black womanhood in the United States. Drawing on literary texts and cultural representations, Richardson shows how five emblematic black women: Mary McLeod Bethune, Rosa Parks, Condoleezza Rice, Michelle Obama, and Beyoncé-have challenged white-centered definitions of American identity.

By using the rhetoric of motherhood and focusing on families and children, these leaders have defied racist images of black women and rewritten scripts of femininity designed to exclude black women from civic participation.

Richardson shows that these women's status as national icons was central to reconstructing Black womanhood in ways that moved beyond dominant stereotypes. However, these formulations are often premised on heteronormativity and exclude Black queer and trans women. Throughout Emancipation's Daughters, Richardson reveals new possibilities for inclusive models of Blackness, national femininity, and democracy.

Emancipation's Daughters Book Reviews

"Riché Richardson has given our tumultuous American moment a brilliant gift. Emancipation's Daughters is an impeccably crafted guide to the struggles, creativity, and iconic labors of African American mothers and their emancipated daughters."
—Houston A. Baker, Distinguished University Professor, Vanderbilt University

"The women Riché Richardson examines broaden notions of Black womanhood in opposition to the dominant imagery perpetuated by filmmakers, advertisers, and other cultural producers in the United States. This broad spectrum of Black womanhood from the early twentieth century to the present allows Richardson to make an expansive argument about the role of these women in the broader American imaginary. The idea of Black women as mothers of the nation outside of the mammy role is a powerful one that has not been framed in the way Richardson does here. Emancipation's Daughters is an engaging and important book."
—Lisa B. Thompson, Beyond the Black Lady: Sexuality and the New African American Middle Class

Emancipation's Daughters: Reimagining Black Femininity and the National Body by Riché Richardson

Riché Richardson, born and raised in Montgomery, Alabama, is a distinguished professor of African American literature at Cornell University's Africana Studies and Research Center since 2008. She earned her Ph.D. in American Literature from Duke University in 1998 and taught at the University of California, Davis from 1998 to 2008.

Her contributions to academia are widely recognized, including being named the 2019-20 Olive B. O'Connor Visiting Distinguished Chair in English at Colgate University. Richardson's notable awards include the 2016 "Educator of the Year Award" from St. Jude Alumni & Friends and being featured on Montgomery artist Bill Ford's series honoring important figures in the city's history.

She is a prolific author with over 40 published essays in prestigious journals like American Literature and Black Renaissance/Renaissance Noire. Her first book, "Black Masculinity and the U.S. South: From Uncle Tom to Gangsta" (2007), received critical acclaim and was honored as an "Outstanding Academic Title." Her latest work, "Emancipation's Daughters: Reimagining Black Femininity and the National Body" (2021), won the 2022 C. Hugh Holman Award from the Society for the Study of Southern Literature (SSSL).

She edited the New Southern Studies Series at the University of Georgia Press from 2018-2022, a book series that has published 25 titles, and for which she has served as the co-editor since 2005, a role in which she now serves alongside Maurice Hobson. She serves on the External Advisory Board of the Black Men's Research Institute at Morehouse College.

Richardson is also a visual artist, known for her mixed-media appliqué art quilts exhibited nationally, including at the Rosa Parks Museum and the Historical Society of Washington, D.C. In 2009, she was honored as a "Cultural Envoy" by the U.S. Embassy in France.

Currently, Richardson is working on her upcoming monograph, "Womanist Worlds: New Southern Voices and Visions in African American Literature," and a critical memoir. Her impactful scholarship and artistic contributions continue to shape conversations surrounding African American culture and literature.

Remembering Daisy Bates, Arkansas and America's Accidental Sojourner for Equality by Janis F. Kearney

Daisy: Between a Rock and a Hard Place by Janis F. Kearney

Janis F. Kearney vividly captures the enduring legacy of civil rights icon Daisy Lee Gatson Bates in her poignant book *Between a Rock and a Hard Place*. As a presidential diarist and esteemed author, Kearney skillfully transforms the life of Daisy Lee Gatson Bates from Black and white to living color.

Drawing from her intimate interviews with Bates, Kearney eloquently traces Bates' remarkable journey from her humble beginnings in the small mill town of Huttig, Arkansas, as an orphaned child, to her pivotal role as one of the most significant southern women civil rights leaders in American history.

Through Kearney's masterful storytelling, readers are immersed in Bates' courageous efforts and unwavering commitment to justice. The book illuminates the struggles and triumphs that defined her extraordinary life. It culminates in a poignant and insightful conversation with Bates during her final days, providing a profound glimpse into the heart and soul of a true civil rights luminary.

"Between a Rock and a Hard Place" is a powerful testament to Bates' enduring legacy and a compelling tribute to her indomitable spirit. With meticulous attention to detail and heartfelt reverence, Janis F. Kearney ensures that Daisy Lee Gatson Bates's extraordinary life is celebrated and remembered for generations to come.

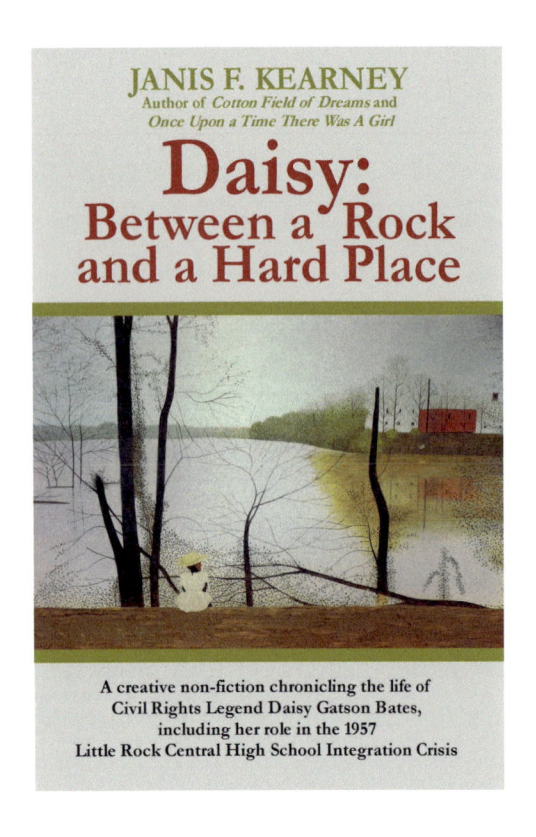

Remembering Daisy Bates, Arkansas and America's Accidental Sojourner for Equality by Janis F. Kearney

Janis F. Kearney is a writer, publisher, and journalist from rural Arkansas. She was raised as the daughter of cotton sharecroppers. Her journey into the world of literature began in the fields of her upbringing, where she developed a profound appreciation for storytelling. With a deep-rooted passion for illuminating the lives of Southerners, Janis crafts narratives spanning short stories, memoirs, autobiographies, biographies, and fiction, reflecting the rich tapestry of her heritage.

Her formal foray into writing commenced in earnest in 2001, following her graduation from the University of Arkansas at Fayetteville with a B.A. in Journalism. Here, she found inspiration from luminaries such as Arkansas Poet Miller Williams, Civil Rights leader Daisy Gatson Bates, and her father, TJ Kearney, who collectively guided her towards a path aimed at effecting positive change through the power of storytelling.

In addition to her endeavors in journalism and publishing, Janis dedicated herself to public service, serving in various capacities in the Clinton Administration from 1993 to 2001. Notably, she held positions such as White House Media Affairs Specialist and Director of Public Communications for the U.S. Small Business Administration and became the first-ever Personal Diarist to a President.

Beyond her professional accomplishments, Janis's commitment to nurturing the next generation of storytellers is evident through her founding of the *Celebrate! Maya Project* in 2014. This nonprofit organization aims to empower young people to find their voices, discover their history, and craft their own narratives through writing workshops, literary competitions, and public forums.

Janis' contributions to literature and journalism have garnered widespread recognition, including her induction into the Arkansas Writers Hall of Fame in 2016 and her 2014 award of the prestigious University of Arkansas Lemke Journalism Award.

Soignée Sisterhood Conversation
Janis F. Kearney

Janis F. Kearney resides in Little Rock, Arkansas, with her husband, Bob Nash. As a proud mother, grandmother, and great-grandmother, Janis inspires and uplifts others through her unwavering dedication to storytelling and advocacy.

In your book, you delve into Daisy Bates' early life in the segregated town of Huttig, Arkansas. Can you share a little of her background and how she became an orphan?
Janis F. Kearney: Daisy Lee Gatson was born in 1914 to a beautiful young couple, Minnie Riley, sixteen, and Hezekiah Gatson, 17, little more than children themselves. Daisy's birth was almost surely an accident of youthful, unchecked love between the unmarried couple, temporary residents of the mill town of Huttig, Arkansas. The rest of Daisy's life journey would somehow echo her accidental existence, her birth in a town that was never home to the child-parents who left her.

Both Millie and Hezekiah were natives of neighboring Louisiana towns. Daisy's biological father, her foster father, and her mother worked for Olin Mill. Most of the Black adults were in some way affiliated with the mill while never being welcomed on the white side of town once their workday ended. Daisy was a toddler when her station in life changed from an over-indulged baby to an orphan. Her young mother was reportedly raped, killed, and dumped in the mill company's pond. It was, in fact, this same pond in which the mill workers transferred logs from one end of the state to the other.

Daisy's father, Hezekiah, left the toddler on the doorsteps of a local millworker and his wife, Oralee, and Susie Smith, before traveling ten miles into Louisiana to make a new life for himself. The Smiths never officially adopted Daisy, even though she was viewed as a very special child. As a child of the Jim Crow era, however, Daisy did not escape the tyranny of racism during these dark days for Blacks.

Can you share some of your early experiences with Mrs. Bates?
Janis F. Kearney: First and foremost, Mrs. Bates will always hold a special place in my heart as my most treasured mentor and the dearest of teachers. Her impact on my life and countless others cannot be overstated, and her legacy as a great American will endure for generations to come.

My journey with Mrs. Bates began when I was just 16 years old and I had the opportunity to work in her office for a summer. Twenty years later, our paths crossed again, and I applied for a job with her. Mrs. Bates remained an influential figure in my life. I'm forever grateful for her unwavering belief in me as a journalist, which paved the way for my eventual role as publisher and owner of the Arkansas State Press.

Daisy Bates faced numerous challenges and threats throughout her life due to her activism. How do you think she found the strength to persevere in the face of such adversity, and what lessons can we learn from her resilience?
Janis F. Kearney: In 1932, Daisy's father was on his deathbed and implored his daughter to forgive and rid herself of her bitterness, in fear it would destroy her. Daisy promised Oralee Smith, the only father she knew, that she would change. And she did. Despite facing immense personal and professional challenges, Daisy Bates remained steadfast in her commitment to justice and equality.

Her resilience stemmed from her unwavering belief in the righteousness of her cause and her determination to create a better future for future generations. Her life teaches us the importance of courage, perseverance, and solidarity in the face of oppression.

Soignée Sisterhood Conversation
Janis F. Kearney

Daisy Bates' role in the Little Rock Central High School Integration Crisis thrust her into the national spotlight. How do you think this experience shaped her legacy, both in Arkansas and across the country?
Janis F. Kearney: In 1954, Daisy Bates was selected as the President of the Arkansas Chapter of the NAACP. It was a surprise selection. She was a 40-year-old female newspaper publisher, but this new role catapulted L.C. and Daisy Bates into becoming Arkansas' foremost power couple. The outspoken editor and publisher of the award-winning Arkansas State Press and the young President of the state's NAACP.

Just two years later, another challenge and opportunity fell into Daisy and L.C. Bates' laps. Little Rock was finally being challenged to uphold the Supreme Court's 1954 Brown vs. Board of Education ruling. Under the guidance of the NAACP's legal counsel Thurgood Marshall, Daisy Bates took on the role as the face and the voice of the 1957 Central High Integration effort and guide for the Little Rock Nine', the children selected to integrate what was Arkansas' most treasured high school.

In your book, you aim to explore Daisy Bates' life beyond her role in the civil rights movement. What lesser-known aspects of her life and personality do you hope readers will discover?
Janis F. Kearney: Daisy Lee Gatson Bates' story is more amazing than fiction. A young girl born in 1914 in the sawmill town of Huttig, Arkansas, her childhood marred by her mother's violent death by whites, her teen years filled with hate, bitterness, and conflicts, and, finally, the transformation into a catalyst for change during America's civil rights struggle. Daisy Bates accidentally catapulted into American history.

She was the fifth recipient of the Margaret Chase Smith Award, the first woman to address the Massachusetts State Senate, tapped as a political adviser to two U.S. Presidents, and cited as the only woman to address the historic March on Washington, led by the Reverend Martin Luther King, Jr.!

How do you think Daisy Bates' experiences reflect broader themes of resilience, agency, and transformation in the face of adversity?
Janis F. Kearney: While many of us cannot think of the Civil Rights movement in Arkansas, the South, or this country without thinking of Daisy Bates, we must never forget that her struggles, challenges, and bravery netted her many disappointments, enemies, and, in time, much sadness. But when asked if she would do it all again, she hurriedly said she would.

Daisy Lee Gatson Bates' journey from a childhood marked by tragedy and discrimination to a prominent civil rights leader embodies the transformative power of resilience and agency. Despite facing overwhelming adversity, she refused to be defined by her circumstances and instead dedicated her life to fighting for justice and equality. Her story is a testament to the indomitable human spirit and the capacity for change, even in the most challenging circumstances.

As an author and activist, how do you hope Daisy Bates' story will continue inspiring future generations? What lessons does her legacy hold for those fighting for justice today?
Janis F. Kearney: Daisy Bates' legacy is a beacon of hope and inspiration for future generations of activists and advocates. Her unwavering commitment to justice and her resilience in the face of adversity serve as a powerful reminder of the importance of speaking truth to power and fighting for what is right. By sharing her story, I hope to inspire others to continue the fight for justice and equality, knowing that even the most ordinary individuals can spark extraordinary change.

Soignée Sisterhood Conversation
Janis F. Kearney

Daisy: Between a Rock and a Hard Place by Janis F. Kearney can be purchased at Amazon.com, Goodreads.com, www.wowpublishing.org and www.janisfkearney.com.

You can visit Janis F. Kearney's social media platforms at:

Website: www.janisfkearney.com
Facebook: www.facebook.com/writingtolearn
LinkedIn: www.linkedin.com/in/janis-f-kearney-8571018

"We've got to decide if it's going to be this generation or never." -- Daisy Lee Gatson Bates (1914-1999) was a civil rights activist, publisher, journalist, and lecturer who played a leading role in the Little Rock Integration Crisis of 1957.

Only on Sundays

Mahalia Jackson's Long Journey
by Janis F. Kearney

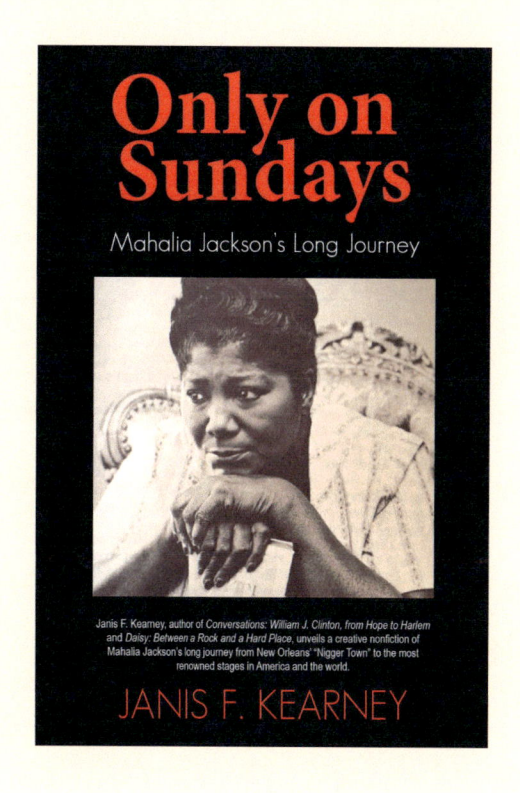

Who was Mahalia Jackson? I began my research of Mahalia Jackson by accident – a dare by former Senator Roland Burris who had purchased her home the same year she passed, in 1972. Fifteen years later, in the midst of the COVID-19 pandemic, I wrote a book about Mahalia Jackson's amazing life journey.

Only on Sundays: Mahalia Jackson's Long Journey is a creative nonfiction that chronicles the years between 1910 - 1972, beginning with Mrs. Jackson's maternal family, the Clarks' migration from the town of Legonier in Pointe Coupee' Parish Louisiana to New Orleans. Seven Clark siblings moved to the uptown community, referred to as "nigger town," because of its predominantly Black populations. The residents were former slaves, children of slaves, sharecroppers and their families migrating from rural Louisiana, and surrounding states.

The Clark family migrated from the Merrick Plantation in Pointe Coupee' Parish, to the poor enclave in New Orleans - one of the few New Orleans communities where poor Blacks could afford to live. The Clark women worked as domestics, cooks, laundresses, and servants for white families, while male siblings worked in manual labor as stevedores on the river ports, or cooks on the river boats.

The Jackson biography paints a vivid portrait of life in New Orleans' most impoverished communities and the Clark family's personal struggles including the loss of Charity, Mahalia's mother, when she was just six years old. Charity's older sister Mahala "Duke," for whom the child was named, "takes on" the girl and her older brother Peter. With that, came the assiduous task of shaping the once-carefree Halie, into the industrious child laborer who contributed to the family's livelihood, which meant her leaving school at 4th grade, and taking on the roles of child-care servant, and laundress at eight. Halie's amazing voice was a gift from God to the world. Aunt Duke often reminded her the gift wasn't to be tainted by New Orleans' street music like Bessie Smith's or Ma Rainey's low-down blues or the Mardi Gras bands that Mahalia fell in love with early in life.

Kearney takes time to revisit the question of what it was that compelled 16 year old Halie to join the Great Migration in 1927, leaving home against her Aunt Duke's wishes, bound for the other Promise Land. A decision that would eventually transform `Little Halie of Nigger town' to Mahalia Jackson, the orphan queen who walked with kings and queens and American royalty and changed the world with her voice.

Only on Sundays can be purchased at Amazon, Goodreads, www.wowpublishing.org and www.janisfkearney.com

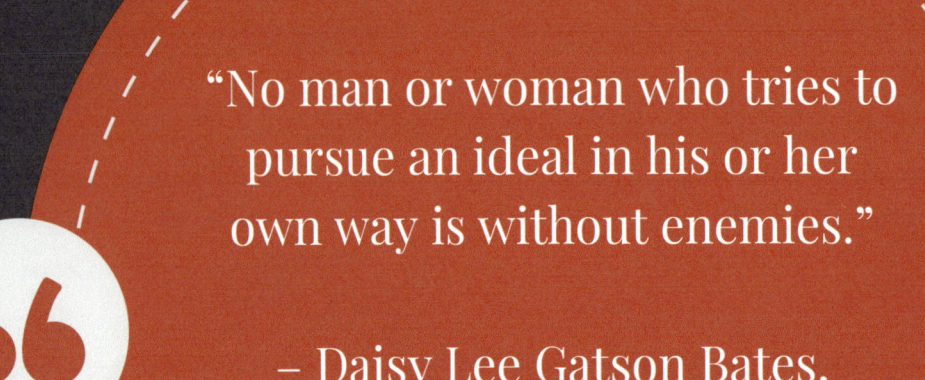

"No man or woman who tries to pursue an ideal in his or her own way is without enemies."

– Daisy Lee Gatson Bates, civil rights activist, publisher, journalist, and lecturer

From Rights to Lives: The Evolution of the Black Freedom Struggle
by Françoise N. Hamlin (Editor) and Charles W. McKinney Jr. (Editor)

Broadly speaking, the traditionally conceptualized mid-twentieth-century Civil Rights Movement and the newer #BlackLivesMatter Movement possess some similar qualities. They both represent dynamic, complex moments of possibility and progress.

They also share mass-based movement activities, policy/legislative advocacy, grassroots organizing, and targeted media campaigns. Innovation, growth, and dissension—core aspects of movement work—mark them both. Crucially, these moments also engender aggressive, repressive, multilevel responses to these assertions of Black humanity.

From Rights to Lives critically engages the dynamic relationship between these two moments of liberatory possibility on the Black Freedom Struggle timeline.

The book's contributors explore what we can learn when we place these moments of struggle in dialogue with each other. They grapple with how our understanding of the postwar moment shapes our analysis of #BLM and wherein lie the discontinuities to glean lessons for future moments of insurgency.

About the Authors

Françoise N. Hamlin is the Royce Family Associate Professor of Teaching Excellence in Africana Studies & History at Brown University. She is the author of the award-winning Crossroads at Clarksdale: The Black Freedom Struggle in the Mississippi Delta after World War II, co-editor of the anthology These Truly Are the Brave: An Anthology of African American Writings on Citizenship and War, and editor and annotator of the republication of The Struggle of Struggles by activist Vera Pigee.

Charles W. McKinney Jr. is chair of Africana studies and associate professor of history at Rhodes College in Memphis, Tennessee. He is the author of Greater Freedom: The Evolution of the Civil Rights Struggle in Wilson, North Carolina, and co-editor of An Unseen Light: Black Struggles for Freedom in Memphis, Tennessee.

Beyond the Black Lady: Sexuality and the New African American Middle Class by Lisa B. Thompson

In this book, Lisa B. Thompson explores the representation of Black middle-class female sexuality by African American women authors in narrative literature, drama, film, and popular culture.

Lisa shows how these depictions reclaim Black female agency and illustrate the difficulties Black women confront in asserting sexual agency in the public sphere.

Thompson broadens the discourse around Black female sexuality by offering an alternate reading of the overly determined racial and sexual script that casts the middle-class "Black lady" as the bastion of African American propriety.

Drawing on the work of Black feminist theorists, she examines symptomatic autobiographies, novels, plays, and key episodes in contemporary American popular culture, including works by Anita Hill, Judith Alexa Jackson, P. J. Gibson, Julie Dash, Kasi Lemmons, Jill Nelson, Lorene Cary, and Andrea Lee.

Praise for Beyond the Black Lady

"[Thompson] finds that some Black women are pioneering new ways to be and to give voice to a more fully actualized, human, female persona. This new woman is long overdue."
— **Diverse: Issues in Higher Education**

"In refreshingly clear prose, Lisa B. Thompson renders a complex and nuanced reading of Black middle-class women from both fiction and real life. This study makes an important intervention in the discourse on what has heretofore been an under-theorized subject."
— **E. Patrick Johnson, author of Sweet Tea: Black Gay Men of the South**

"A path-breaking, cogently argued, bold study of the ways in which Black women writers and public figures have engaged, confronted, resisted, or overturned prevailing notions of Black middle-class women's sexuality. This book makes a powerful contribution to debates in race studies, gender and sexuality studies, performance studies, and literary and cultural studies."
— **Valerie Smith, author of Not Just Race, Not Just Gender: Black Feminist Readings**

Available for purchase from Amazon, Barnes and Noble and the University of Illinois Press

Beyond the Black Lady: Sexuality and the New African American Middle Class by Lisa B. Thompson

Lisa B. Thompson is a professor of African and African Diaspora Studies at the University of Texas at Austin. She is the author of three books, Beyond The Black Lady: Sexuality and the New African American Middle Class (University of Illinois Press, 2009), Single Black Female (Samuel French Inc., 2012), and Underground, Monroe, and The Mamalogues: Three Plays (Northwestern University Press, 2020).

Her scholarship focuses on identity, representation, and performance issues in contemporary African American culture. Thompson's award-winning plays, which have been produced off-Broadway throughout the US and internationally, explore African American history and culture through the lens of the middle class.

Professor Thompson's teaching has been recognized by the Texas Exes and the Warfield Center for African and African American Studies. Her work has received support from the American Council of Learned Societies; Harvard University's W.E.B. DuBois Research Institute; the University of Texas at Austin Humanities Institute; the Michele R. Clayman Institute for Gender Research; the University of California's Office of the President; the Five Colleges; Stanford University's Center for Comparative Studies in Race and Ethnicity; Hedgebrook; the Millay Colony for the Arts; and MacDowell.

She co-hosts and co-produces Black Austin Matters, a podcast and radio segment on KUT, Austin's NPR station, that explores Black life, culture, and politics in Central Texas.

Lisa B. Thompson is currently the Bobby and Sherri Patton Professor of African and African Diaspora Studies at the Department of Theatre & Dance and the College of Liberal Arts' Advisor to the Dean for Faculty Mentoring and Support at the University of Texas at Austin.

#SayHerName: Black Women's Stories of Police Violence and Public Silence by Kimberlé Crenshaw

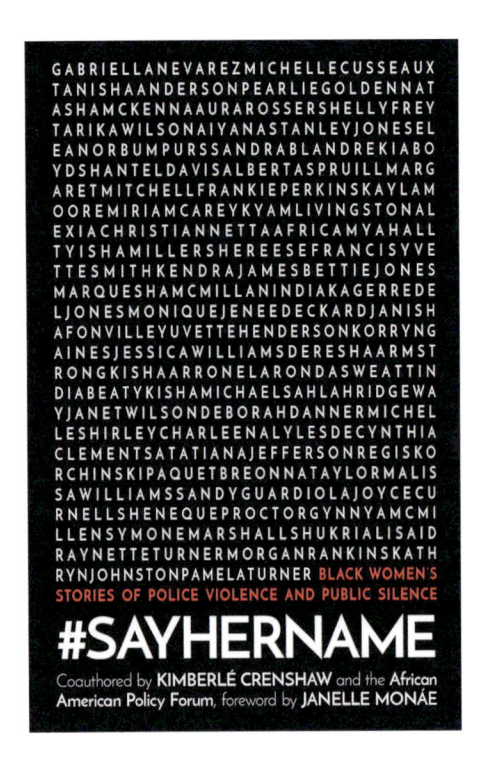

"Kimberlé Crenshaw is a national treasure."
— Kerry Washington

"The United States does not value Black life—and white supremacy threatens all of humanity. The Black women's stories of state violence and public silence featured in this powerful and inspiring book are extremely important. We bear children, so when they are robbed from us, it's like our own breath is taken away. We thank the #SayHerName campaign and Kimberlé Crenshaw and Janelle Monáe for uplifting our stories. The African American Policy Forum is a vital platform for Black voices."

— Samaria Rice, founder, Tamir Rice Foundation, and mother of Tamir Rice

Fill the void. Lift your voice. Say Her Name.
Black women, girls, and femmes as young as seven and as old as ninety-three have been killed by the police, though we rarely hear their names or learn their stories. Breonna Taylor, Alberta Spruill, Rekia Boyd, Shantel Davis, Shelly Frey, Kayla Moore, Kyam Livingston, Miriam Carey, Michelle Cusseaux, and Tanisha Anderson are among the many lives that should have been.

#SayHerName provides an analytical framework for understanding Black women's susceptibility to police brutality and state-sanctioned violence, and it explains how—through Black feminist storytelling and ritual—we can effectively mobilize various communities and empower them to advocate for racial justice.

Centering Black women's experiences in police violence and gender violence discourses sends the powerful message that, in fact, all Black lives matter and that the police cannot kill without consequence. This is a powerful story of Black feminist practice, community-building, enablement, and Black feminist reckoning.

About The African American Policy Forum
Founded in 1996, The African American Policy Forum is an innovative think tank that connects academics, activists and policy-makers to promote efforts to dismantle structural inequality. We utilize new ideas and innovative perspectives to transform public discourse and policy. AAPF promotes frameworks and strategies that address a vision of racial justice that embraces the intersections of race, gender, class, and the array of barriers that disempower those who are marginalized in society. AAPF is dedicated to advancing and expanding racial justice, gender equality, and the indivisibility of all human rights, both in the United States and internationally.

#SayHerName: Black Women's Stories of Police Violence and Public Silence by Kimberlé Crenshaw

Kimberlé W. Crenshaw is a pioneering scholar and writer on civil rights, critical race theory, Black feminist legal theory, and race, racism, and the law. In addition to her position at Columbia Law School, she is a Distinguished Professor of Law at the University of California, Los Angeles.

Crenshaw coined the terms "Intersectionality" and "Critical Race Theory" and has been a leading voice in the fight against intersectional violence. Her influential work on intersectionality played a pivotal role in the drafting of the equality clause in the South African Constitution.

At the United Nations World Conference on Racism in 2001, Crenshaw authored the background paper on race and gender discrimination and served as the rapporteur for the conference's expert group on gender and race discrimination. She also coordinated NGO efforts to ensure gender inclusion in the conference declaration.

Through her scholarship, writing, and activism, Crenshaw has shed light on key issues perpetuating inequality, including the "school-to-prison pipeline" for African American children and the criminalization of behavior among Black teenage girls.

She co-founded the Columbia Law School African American Policy Forum (AAPF) and authored "*Say Her Name: Resisting Police Brutality Against Black Women*" to draw attention to police violence against Black women and girls.

She co-authored "*Black Girls Matter: Pushed Out, Overpoliced, and Underprotected*" and has contributed to prestigious legal journals.

In 1981, she assisted Anita Hill's legal team during her testimony at the confirmation hearing of Supreme Court Justice Clarence Thomas.

Crenshaw writes regularly for The New Republic, The Nation, and Ms. and provides commentary for media outlets, including MSNBC and NPR, and hosts the podcast *Intersectionality Matters!*

In addition to frequent speaking engagements, training sessions, and town halls, Crenshaw has facilitated workshops for human rights activists in Brazil and in India and for constitutional court judges in South Africa.

Advertise With Us!

$175 per full page

scan to learn more

SOIGNÉE

Reading Challenge

Log into Facebook and scan the QR code to join us on the Black Pearls Magazine Facebook Fan Page

Crown Holders Read!

Book-A-Week Reading Challenge

Crown Holders Book-A-Week Reading Challenge

We are asking our readers to join us in a year-long reading challenge. Each week we will read a new book and discuss it on the Black Pearls Magazine Facebook fan page. Log into Facebook and scan the QR code below. Under each book listed on our page, feel free to leave your thoughts, comments, questions, and book reviews. We welcome all book lovers!

Each year thousands of people and educators, concerned parents, community leaders, authors, poets, personal development coaches and publishers devote their time and resources to presenting the reader with great books! However, too many outstanding books do not get the attention and reader support that they deserve.

It is our mission at Crown Holders Transmedia and Soignée Lifestyle Publications to connect readers with these hidden gems and bring them books that will impact their lives. Please scan the QR code and visit all of our bookstore shelves and share the reading lists with your friends.

Scan the QR code to shop for new books at our bespoke online bookstore or visit our reading lists at www.amazon.com/shop/edc1creations. There are books for the entire family including poetry books, science fiction, crime thrillers, bibles, faith-filled fiction, business & self-help books, non-fiction, children's books, cookbooks, and even history books.

Scan & Shop

"One of the many gifts that books give readers is a connection to each other. When we share an affection for a writer, an author or a story, we also have a better understanding of people unlike ourselves. Books cultivate empathy." — Sarah Jessica Parker

02 *Soignée*

Sisters Tap In

"Take an oath. Make a promise. Declare a commitment. You will refrain from being the same person month on month and take imperial steps each day to become your next infinite version."
― Hiral Nagda

Sister, Are You Ready To Tap-in?

This "Sisters Tap-in" section is a reservoir of wisdom and actionable steps, a sanctuary where women prioritize their mental, spiritual, and physical well-being. Straightforward guidance on setting boundaries, fostering self-love, and navigating the complexities of empowerment await.

This is a rallying point for sisters in the pursuit of authenticity, healing, and an unshakable sense of safety. Ready to tap into your power? Let's dive in.

↬ Navigate anger through constructive means. Whether it's putting pen to paper or engaging in physical activity, embrace outlets that allow you to express and comprehend your emotions. Please don't shy away from seeking therapy when necessary, as it creates a supportive space for emotional well-being.

↬ In the pursuit of balance, moderation becomes a guiding principle. Cultivate a sense of equilibrium across various facets of life, from work and relationships to self-care. This moderation serves as the cornerstone for feeling complete and secure in your mental, spiritual, and physical well-being.

↬ Elevate your relationship with food through mindfulness. Savor every bite, seeing it as nourishment rather than a mere coping mechanism. This shift in perspective fosters physical well-being and nurtures a positive connection with your body.

↬ Shift the narrative within; replace self-criticism with self-compassion. Recognize your inherent worth and extend this culture of support to your relationships. Emphasize constructive communication for mutual growth, fostering an environment of understanding.

Surviving Life's Punches: 20 Reminders for When Everything Sucks

Life can be challenging. It's a rollercoaster of highs and lows, twists and turns that can sometimes leave us feeling overwhelmed and lost. In those moments, reminders are important to help us navigate the challenges with resilience and grace.

Here are 20 daily reminders to lean on when life gets tough:

1. This, too, shall pass. No storm lasts forever.
2. Embracing imperfections makes you human.
3. Focus on progress, not perfection.
4. Every setback is an opportunity for growth.
5. Make peace with what you cannot change.
6. Practice self-care rituals that nourish your soul.
7. Find something to be thankful for each day.
8. Set boundaries to protect your mental health.
9. You've overcome challenges before; you can do it again.
10. Surround yourself with positivity.
11. Small steps forward are still progress.
12. Find inspiration in stories of perseverance.
13. You are stronger than you think.
14. Reach out for support when you need it.
15. Remember that setbacks are not failures; they're lessons.
16. Rest when you need to recharge.
17. Take breaks from technology to reconnect with yourself.
18. Tomorrow is a new day with new possibilities.
19. Keep faith in brighter days ahead.
20. Celebrate your victories, no matter how small.

Surviving Life's Punches: 20 Reminders for When Everything Sucks

Life can indeed be a formidable opponent, striking us with unexpected blows that leave us reeling and gasping for air. Just when we think we've found our footing, another punch comes hurtling our way, threatening to knock us down for good. In those moments when it feels like the entire world is crumbling around us, it's easy to succumb to feelings of despair, hopelessness, and defeat

But here's the thing: even in the midst of chaos and uncertainty, there is strength within you that you may not even realize exists. You are far more resilient than you give yourself credit for. Despite the relentless barrage of punches, you have the power to rise up, dust yourself off, and keep fighting.

Think of yourself as a boxer in the ring, facing off against the challenges of life with courage and determination. With each blow that lands, you may stumble and falter, but you refuse to stay down. You dig deep, drawing upon a wellspring of inner strength and resilience that propels you forward, even in the face of adversity.

And remember, you are not alone in this fight. There are people who care about you, believe in you, and are willing to stand by your side through thick and thin. Reach out to them for support when you need it, lean on them for strength when you feel weak, and draw inspiration from their unwavering faith in your ability to overcome. In those moments when everything seems bleak and hopeless, hold onto the glimmer of hope that burns within you. Remind yourself that every challenge you face is an opportunity for growth, every setback is a stepping stone toward success, and every punch that life throws your way only strengthens you.

So, stand tall, my friend. Square your shoulders, lift your chin, and face life's challenges head-on with courage, resilience, and unwavering determination. You are stronger than you think, and no matter how tough the fight may be, you have what it takes to emerge victorious in the end.

Jaachynma N.E. Agu, My Heritage

"Balanced Life Is About Quality of Time At Work, Quantity of Time At Home And Staying Connected To God All The Time!"

IT IS MY *Time*

Embracing Your Season: Soignée Womanhood

Isn't it incredible how we've reclaimed our voices? Our voices echo through literature, art, music, and activism, reminding the world that we are here, and our stories matter. We inspire, educate, and empower, showing what it means to rise above challenges and live out our dreams as a Black Woman, a Soignée Woman.

You know, there's something truly magical about being a Black Woman! We've earned the privilege to share our truths unapologetically and without hesitation. Think about it. Our journeys, colored by the shades of our skin and the richness of our heritage, have created this beautiful mosaic of experiences. We've been through ups and downs, faced adversity head-on, and emerged stronger and wiser.

Remember this: your past and pain, intertwined with trauma, questionable choices, and generational struggles, do not define you. Let's be open and transparent, confronting the distractions with courage and preparing to embrace the triumphant future that awaits, guided by the divine. God, in His infinite grace, provides tools to recognize the impact of your experiences, urging you to see yourself through His eyes.

Healing is a journey of progression, not perfection, and you're well on your way. Regardless of the mistakes and the depths of pain, nothing can diminish the God-given value of your life. It's a transformative moment—to turn your damage into destiny! You may bear scars, but you are far from being destroyed. Embrace the moment in time, this season, with joy, joy, unspeakable joy!

Affirmations

Empowered, Unstoppable and Flourishing You!

Repeat these affirmations regularly, allowing them to sink into your consciousness and become a powerful tool for cultivating a mindset of empowerment, resilience, and growth. Embrace the unique qualities that make you unstoppable and let these affirmations inspire you to flourish!

01 Flourishing

"My life is a garden of growth and abundance; I flourish in the sunlight of positivity, nurturing the blossoming aspects of my being."

02 Empowered

"I harness the incredible power within me to shape my reality, confidently navigating my journey."

03 Authenticity

Rooted in authenticity, I flourish. Adversity morphs into opportunities, nurturing my growth. Each setback is a testament to my inner strength. In this garden of self-discovery, I bloom—radiant, authentic, and flourishing.

04 Unstoppable

I have become an unstoppable force. Challenges are stepping stones to triumph. I journey fearlessly. Adversity fuels growth, and I emerge victorious—unstoppable and true to myself.

Affirmations

Empowered, Unstoppable and Flourishing You!

05 Palpable Energy

My energy is palpable! A radiant aura precedes me, a magnetic field of positivity and authenticity that leaves an indelible imprint on the hearts of those who encounter me.

06 Processing

Making time to process strong emotions is a sacred ritual. I honor the depth of my feelings, embracing the transformative power of emotional awareness as I navigate the ebb and flow of life.

07 Evolving

Discipline births peace within. With a commitment to self-growth, I forge a path where disciplined choices lead to inner tranquility. In this disciplined peace, I find serenity.

08 Safety and Support

Choosing connections that provide safety and support, I set out on a quest for genuine bonds. I blossom in the refuge of understanding people, knowing the sanctuary of true companionship envelops me.

09 Exhalation

Inhaling dreams, I exhale fears—a transformative breath of liberation. Each exhales the shackles of doubt, making space for the manifestation of aspirations. With each breath, I cultivate a fearless tomorrow where dreams materialize.

"Owning our story can be hard but not nearly as difficult as spending our lives running from it."
— Brené Brown

4 Unique Ways to Nourish Your Mind, Body, and Soul Spiritually

"I am a feminist, and what that means to me is much the same as the meaning of the fact that I am Black; it means that I must undertake to love myself and to respect myself as though my very life depends upon self-love and self-respect." **– June Jordan**

It's easy to get lost in the hustle and bustle of daily life, and we need to remember to take care of ourselves. When it comes to nurturing our minds, bodies, and souls, many of us turn to meditation, nature, journaling, or connecting with others. While these practices are undoubtedly beneficial, they may only resonate with some. The good news is that many other holistic ways to care for yourself spiritually exist. Here are four unique ways to nourish your mind, body, and soul that do not involve connecting with others.

Sound Healing
Sound healing is an ancient practice that uses sound vibrations to promote relaxation, reduce stress, and heal the body. It involves listening to specific sounds or tones that are believed to have a therapeutic effect on the mind and body. These sounds can come from various sources, such as singing bowls, gongs, chimes, or even the human voice. Sound healing can be practiced alone or with a trained practitioner, and it is said to promote a deep sense of inner peace and well-being.

Art Therapy
Art therapy is a form of therapy that uses art-making to promote self-expression, emotional healing, and personal growth. It involves creating art as a way to process and express emotions, thoughts, and experiences. Art therapy can be practiced individually or in a group setting and does not require artistic talent or skill. It is said to be a powerful tool for reducing stress, anxiety, and depression and improving overall mental health.

Movement Therapy
Movement therapy is a form of therapy that uses physical movement as a way to promote emotional and psychological well-being. It involves moving the body in various ways, such as dance, yoga, or tai chi, to release tension, reduce stress, and improve mood. Movement therapy can be practiced alone or with a trained practitioner, and it is said to promote a deep sense of connection between the mind, body, and spirit.

Aromatherapy
Aromatherapy is a holistic healing practice that uses essential oils to promote physical, emotional, and spiritual well-being. It involves using plant-based oils, such as lavender, peppermint, or eucalyptus, to create a relaxing and soothing atmosphere.

Essential oils can be used in various ways, such as diffusing them into the air, adding them to bathwater, or applying them to the skin. Aromatherapy reduces stress, promotes relaxation, and improves overall mood and well-being.

These four unique practices – sound healing, art therapy, movement therapy, and aromatherapy – offer alternative ways to nourish your mind, body, and soul. Give them a try and see how they can enhance your spiritual well-being. Remember, self-care is essential, and exploring different methods is okay until you find what works best for you.

Be Your Best

"As much as we can fight for material-related dreams, we must also fight for intangible progression in terms of improving ourselves.

Financial success is important but it doesn't supersede the success of being the best version of yourself.

Fight for that, live for that, it will make you powerful, be the best version of yourself."
— Tare Munzara

Let Love Navigate, Bliss Awaits

What does the intertwining of love and happiness mean to you in daily life?

Love and happiness, like trusted companions, work together to shape a vibrant existence, unfolding in the simplicity of shared laughter and comforting embraces. Love becomes the compass that steers us through life's unpredictable turns, while happiness, the radiant sun, warms our days with its golden glow.

In the company of those who cherish our authentic selves, each day transforms into a jubilant celebration of shared joy. The innocent laughter of children, the resonance of heartfelt conversations, and the embrace of simple pleasures elevate the ordinary into the extraordinary. Love, a steadfast companion, nurtures hearts to blossom and souls to flourish in the journey of life.

Happiness, a constant companion in life's journey, extends an invitation to sway with the rhythmic dance of the present moment. Whether discovered in the serenity of nature, the indulgence of a delicious meal, or the warmth of a sunbeam on our skin, happiness paints vibrant hues onto life's canvas.

Love and happiness, intricately entwined, collaboratively work together to shape the fabric of our days, weaving threads of contentment and fulfillment.

Allow love to be your guiding star, and let happiness be your cherished destination. Together, they create moments saturated with peace and joy, making every step and every moment a celebration of the extraordinary!

If the path ahead appears unclear, remember that sometimes, you must forge your own way, guided by the love within and enveloped by the happiness that surrounds you!

Triumph Over Self-Sabotage

"We can be redeemed only to the extent to which we see ourselves." — Martin Buber

Triumph Over Self-Sabotage

Challenge and overcome self-sabotaging and negative mindsets

01 Start by identifying and acknowledging your self-sabotaging behaviors. Without acknowledgement, it will be difficult to make any changes. Once you've identified them, you can start to reframe them.

02 Challenge your negative thoughts and reframe them into more positive ones. A way to challenge your negative thoughts is to question them. Why are you thinking this? Is there evidence to support it? If not, then it might not be worth your worry.

03 Work on building up your self-confidence and self-esteem. There are many things we can do to improve our self-confidence and self-esteem. By taking steps to improve our mental state, we can lead happier and more successful lives. We can do this by setting goals, working on positive self-talk, and by seeking help when needed.

04 If you can learn to be more gentle and understanding with yourself, you will find that your self-esteem improves, you become more productive, and your overall outlook on life becomes more positive.

05 Commit to your happiness by making a conscious effort to do things that make you joyful. Find out what makes you truly fulfilled and then make a plan to incorporate those things into your life. It means making yourself a priority and taking care of yourself, both mentally and physically.

03
Soignée

Embrace Your Tribe

"A tribe is a group of people connected to one another, connected to a leader, and connected to an idea. For millions of years, human beings have been part of one tribe or another. A group needs only two things to be a tribe: a shared interest and a way to communicate." - Seth Godin

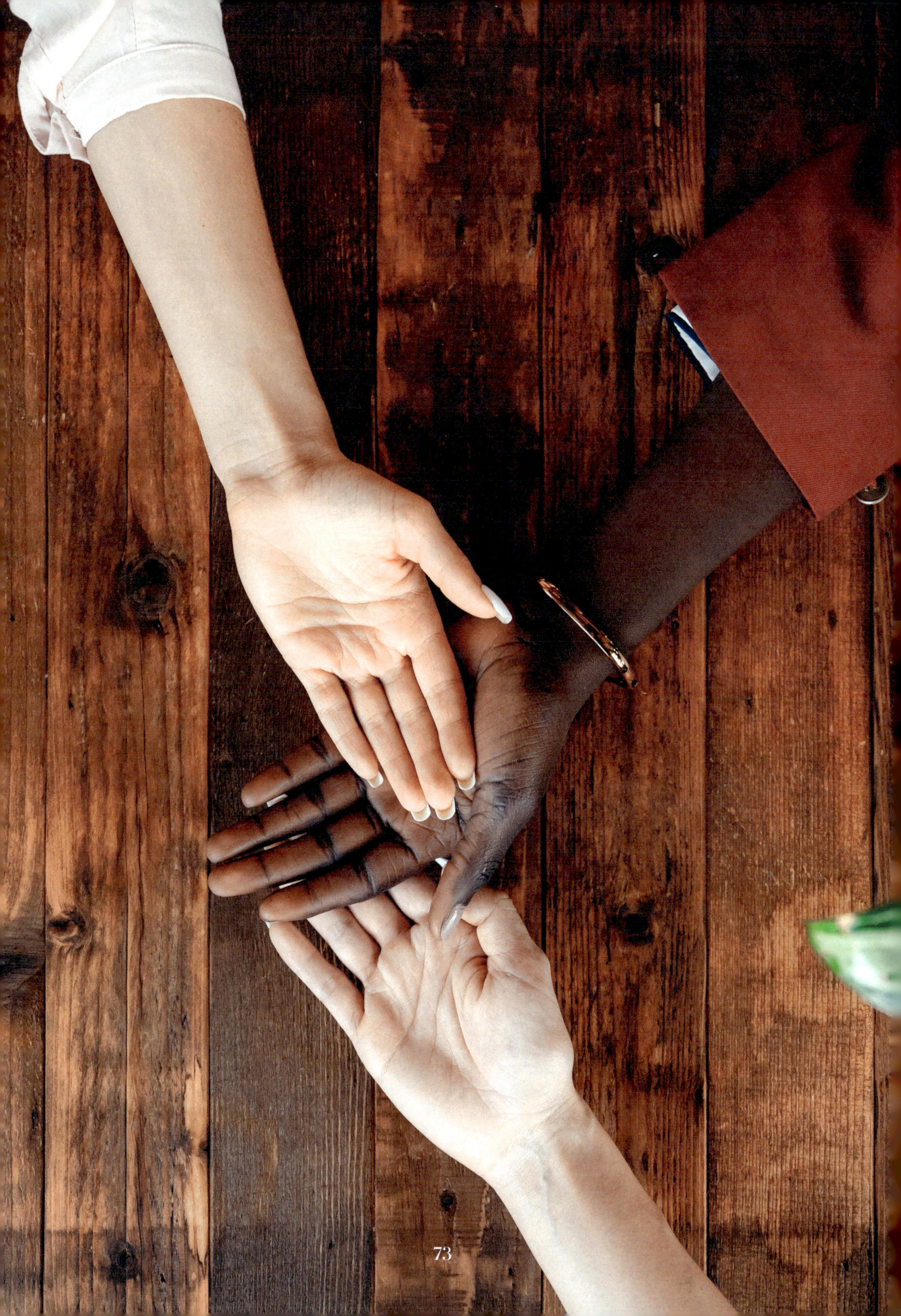

Crown Holders Sisterhood on Facebook

This month, nurture your relationships with your global sisterhood.

We are the Daughters of Zora, Maya, Toni, and Terry—a supportive community empowering women to launch their dream projects or businesses. Welcoming all women, including book reviewers, podcasters, solopreneurs, educators, fashionistas, activists, coaches, writers, influencers, vloggers, mom bosses, and leaders. Our mission is to help each sister activate their dreams and enrich their lives. Our diverse community shares inspirational wisdom, personal stories, daily affirmations, and practical tools through audio/video classes to advance our lives and careers. Join us in this safe space and let's thrive together.

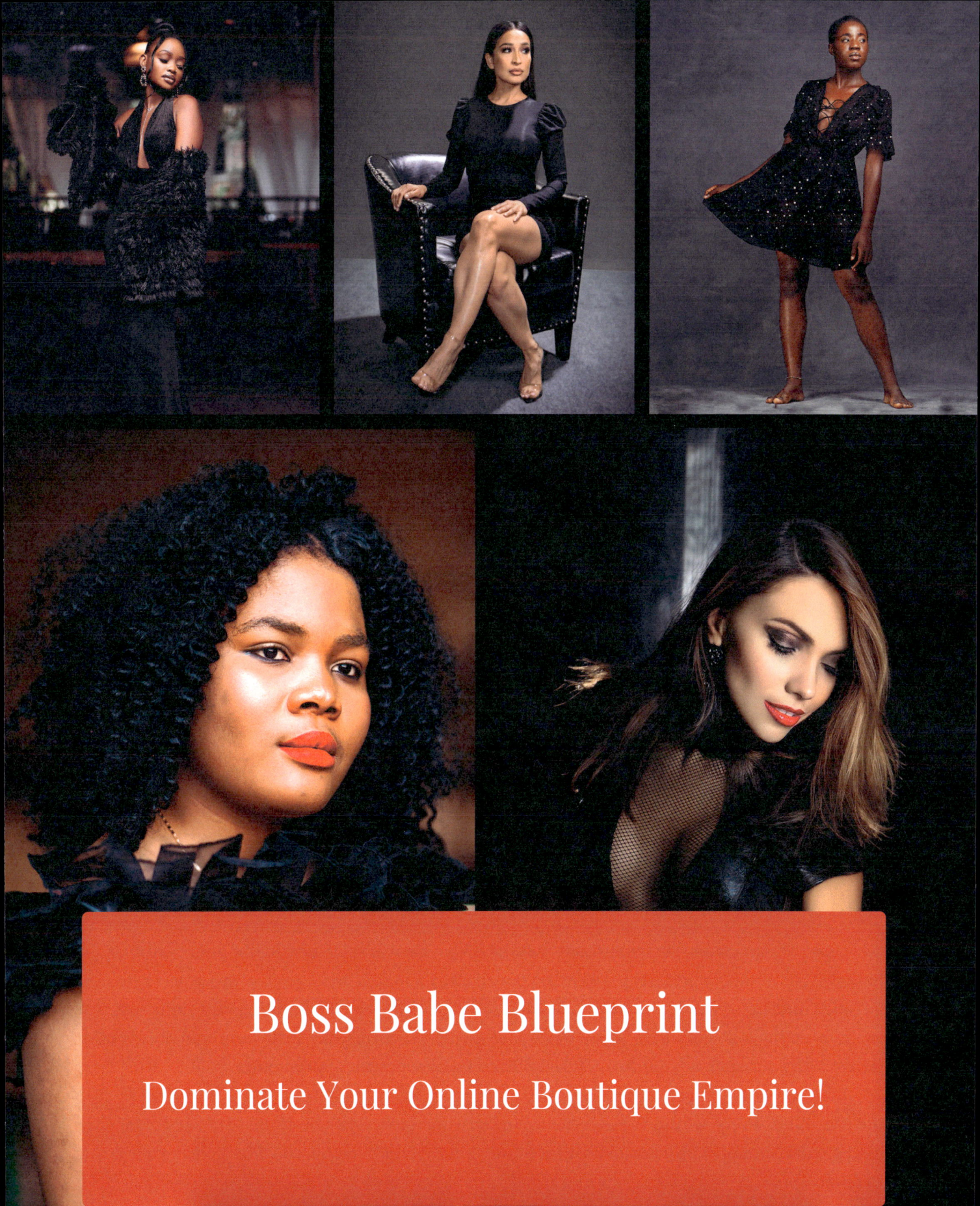

Boss Babe Blueprint

Dominate Your Online Boutique Empire!

Boss Babe Blueprint: Dominate Your Online Boutique Empire!

Starting an online boutique is an exciting endeavor that requires practical planning, savvy decision-making, and careful consideration of funding. Let's dive in with some down-to-earth advice to help you kickstart your boutique opening!

First off, acknowledge the challenges you might face, like managing your budget and dealing with potential setbacks. Securing funding for your venture is crucial, whether it's through personal savings, loans, or investment from friends and family. Be sure to budget carefully, accounting for expenses like inventory, marketing, website development, and any other operational costs. Additionally, explore funding options such as small business grants or crowdfunding platforms to supplement your initial capital.

But don't let funding worries discourage you! With a clear understanding of your target audience and a solid business plan in place, you'll be ready to tackle whatever comes your way. Consider starting small and gradually scaling up as your business grows to minimize financial risk. Remember, Rome wasn't built in a day, and neither will your boutique be.

Now, let's talk logistics. Setting up shop online means you'll need to find reliable vendors for your products. Look for suppliers who offer quality items at a fair price and can deliver them on time. Building good relationships with your vendors will be key to keeping your inventory stocked and your customers happy. Consider attending trade shows or reaching out to wholesalers to discover new suppliers and expand your product offerings.

As you start making sales, keep a close eye on your performance. Pay attention to metrics like website traffic, sales numbers, and customer feedback. This data will help you identify what's working well and where you might need to make adjustments. Use tools like Google Analytics or Shopify's built-in analytics to track your progress and make informed decisions about your business strategy.

Slow times are inevitable in any business, but they don't have to spell disaster for your boutique. Use these periods as an opportunity to reassess your strategy and find creative ways to attract customers. Consider offering special promotions, hosting virtual events, or collaborating with influencers to generate excitement and drive sales. Use social media platforms like Instagram and Facebook to engage with your audience and keep them updated on new arrivals or promotions.

And remember, every setback is just a chance to learn and grow. Don't be afraid to try new things and take calculated risks. With a positive attitude and a willingness to adapt, you'll be well on your way to success.

So, roll up your sleeves and get ready to bring your boutique to life! With a little determination, strategic planning, and a lot of passion, you'll soon be celebrating your grand opening and welcoming customers to your stylish online haven. Best of luck on your boutique journey!

Pamela Samuels Young's Tips for Pursuing Your Passion

Put in the Time - I meet people who have a dream but expect it to come to fruition at the snap of their fingers. The reality is that it takes time. I completed my first novel by waking at four in the morning to write for a couple of hours before work. It took me three years to finish my first book, and then I couldn't find an agent. I didn't give up. I wrote a second novel, *Every Reasonable Doubt*, which started my writing career. Anything worth having is worth working for.

Master Your Craft - Concentrate on learning your craft. When I finished my first book, I knew it would be a bestseller. I still have that manuscript, and it sucks! Learning how to craft and plot a mystery novel took time and study. Take courses, research your passion online, and practice, practice, practice. Make sure you're really as good as you think you are.

Join Professional Organizations—Surround yourself with others who share your passion. Hundreds of professional organizations' sole function is to help their members develop their creative talents and realize their business goals. I belong to Sisters in Crime, Mystery Writers of America, and Romance Writers of America, which have been instrumental in my success as a writer. No matter your passion, there's bound to be a networking group you can join.

Ignore the Naysayers - People who don't have the motivation to pursue their own dreams will often try to derail yours. People repeatedly discouraged me when I told them I planned to give up my law career to write mystery novels. I also received over a dozen rejection letters before finally landing my first agent.

Once I finally landed a book deal, there was still more rejection. After Harlequin published *Every Reasonable Doubt* and *In Firm Pursuit*, which were both Essence magazine bestsellers, nine publishing houses rejected my third book, *Murder on the Down Low*. That left me no option but to self-publish, which was the best decision I ever made for my writing career.

My novel *Anybody's Daughter* won the NAACP Image Award for Outstanding Fiction against four bestselling authors at major publishing houses (Walter Mosley, Terry McMillan, Sistah Soljah, and Victoria Christopher Murray).

Later, two publishing houses that had previously rejected my work were interested in publishing me. Their outreach was a major validating moment. All the rejection I experienced taught me to take charge of my own writing career. I'm now happily self-published and writing full-time.

Pamela Samuels Young, an award-winning author and attorney, hails from Compton, California, where she developed a passion for setting and achieving ambitious goals. With a background in labor and employment law, she served as Managing Counsel for Toyota in Southern California for fifteen years while simultaneously pursuing her passion for writing. Her journey as a mystery writer began with early morning sessions before work, leading to a successful career as a full-time author.

Committed to both entertaining and educating her readers, she aims to spark meaningful conversations through her work. Pamela is also the author of "*The Law of Karma*," "*Sounds Like a Plan*," and "*Kinky Coily: A Natural Hair Resource Guide*." A sought-after speaker on self-empowerment and fiction writing, she resides in the Los Angeles area.

PARTNER
With Us!

Partner with Soignée Lifestyle Magazine

Promote Your Excellence. Share Your Story. Amplify Your Presence!

Are you ready to shine a spotlight on your product, service, book, or business? Look no further – Soignée Lifestyle Magazine offers you the perfect platform to showcase your talents! Join us in a celebration of positivity and creativity, reaching a diverse audience eager to discover and support remarkable ventures.

Why Partner with Soignée?

Diverse Audience - Our magazine attracts a wide and diverse readership, including individuals, churches, book store owners, librarians, book clubs and women's groups, creators, bloggers, and podcasters. Your message will reach an engaged community with a positive mindset.

Positive Vibes Only - We welcome content, products, and services that spread positivity, inspiration, and empowerment. Do you have a product or service that solves a problem? Could you align your brand with a magazine that values uplifting narratives and fosters a community of support for entrepreneurs? Sure you can!

Affordable Display - For just $175.00, you can secure a full-color page in our magazine. Benefit from cost-effective advertising that maximizes your visibility and impact. We can create your page or you can create your own! Your advertisement will appear in our print magazine and be featured in the digital version, reaching an even broader audience across various platforms.

Community Support - By advertising with Soignée, you become a part of our supportive community. Connect with like-minded individuals and businesses, fostering relationships that extend beyond a single advertisement.

How to Advertise in Soignée Lifestyle Magazine

Contact Us - Email us at elladcurry@edc-creations.com to express your interest in advertising with Soignée Lifestyle Magazine. We will let you know our themes and what we have open to showcase your company.

Submit Your Content - Make your payment of $175.00 to secure a full-color page in our upcoming issue. Please provide us with your eye-catching content, ensuring it aligns with our positive and empowering ethos. If you need us to create your ad, don't hesitate to let us know. We are here to help as much as needed.

Get Featured - Watch your business, product, or service gain visibility in both our print and digital editions, captivating the hearts of our diverse readership. We promote all advertisers on our social media for 60 days!

Partner with Soignée Lifestyle Magazine and Let Your Gifts Shine!

Join us in spreading positive messages, supporting vibrant ventures, and celebrating the richness of diversity. Advertise with Soignée, where your story becomes a part of a thriving community eager to embrace and champion your excellence! Spread the word to other business owners; we are here to uplift others as we grow.

Connect with us today by scanning the QR code in the back of the magazine.

Unlocking Financial Freedom

A MILLENNIAL'S GUIDE TO SMART MONEY MOVES

Unlocking Financial Freedom

A Millennial's Guide to Smart Money Moves

It's no secret that navigating the financial landscape can be daunting, especially in today's fast-paced world. But fear not, because we're about to unlock a few tips to financial freedom and set you on a path toward a secure and prosperous future.

Embrace Financial Literacy: Financial freedom starts with understanding that money matters. Take the time to educate yourself about budgeting, investing, and the basics of personal finance. Numerous online resources, podcasts, and books cater specifically to millennials, making it easier than ever to boost your financial IQ.

Practicing Mindful Spending and Strategic Debt Management: Differentiate between wants and needs as you strive for financial freedom. Effectively manage debts by prioritizing high-interest ones and exploring options such as consolidation or refinancing to reduce interest payments. Utilize tools like direct deposit and autopay to ensure timely bill payments, preventing the temptation to overspend before settling essential expenses.

Create a Budget That Works for You: Crafting a budget is the cornerstone of financial success. Tailor it to your lifestyle, accounting for both necessities and discretionary spending. Apps like Mint, Honeydue, Goodbudget, PocketGuard, or You Need a Budget (YNAB) can help you track expenses and set realistic financial goals.

Tackle Student Loans Strategically: Many millennials bear the weight of student loans, but there are strategic ways to manage this burden. Investigate loan consolidation or refinancing options to lower interest rates. Additionally, explore income-driven repayment plans that align with your financial situation.

Invest Early and Wisely: Time is your greatest asset when it comes to investing. Take advantage of compounding interest by starting to invest early. Diversify your portfolio and consider low-cost index funds or robo-advisors for a hands-off approach to building wealth. Here are a few great places for beginning investors to get started: Acorns, Stash, Robinhood, Betterment, Charles Schwab, and SoFi Invest. Do your research and limit yourself at first!

Explore Side Hustles: In the gig economy era, opportunities for side hustles abound. Whether it's freelance work, consulting, or starting a small business, additional income streams can accelerate your journey to financial freedom. Here are a few websites to explore: Thumbtack, TaskRabbit, Upwork, Behance, Freelancer, 99designs, Instacart, and Clarity.

Prioritize Emergency Savings: Life is unpredictable, and having a financial safety net is crucial. Aim to save three to six months' worth of living expenses in an easily accessible account. This emergency fund provides peace of mind and financial stability during unexpected challenges.

Unlocking Financial Freedom

A Millennial's Guide to Smart Money Moves

Leverage Employer Benefits: Take full advantage of employer-sponsored benefits, such as 401(k) matching programs or health savings accounts (HSAs). These perks can significantly enhance your financial position and set you on the path to long-term wealth accumulation.

Plan for Future Homeownership
Owning a home marks a significant milestone for many millennials, symbolizing financial stability and the fulfillment of long-term goals. As you start down this path, it's essential to broaden your perspective beyond the initial step of exploring loan options.

When buying a new home, consider future resale value. Attend open houses to get a feel for different properties. Inspect homes thoroughly, considering potential maintenance costs. Work with a reputable real estate agent and negotiate wisely. Factor in additional expenses like property taxes and homeowners insurance. Please make sure the home aligns with your future plans and lifestyle. Be patient and wait for the right opportunity.

Discuss Credit Scores with Potential Partners or Spouses: Before entering into homeownership, it's crucial to have open and honest conversations about all debt and credit scores with potential partners or spouses. A good credit score is instrumental in securing favorable loan terms, and understanding each other's financial standing is vital. This discussion can pave the way for joint financial planning and help set realistic expectations for the homebuying process.

Research Areas and New Developments: The location of your future home plays a pivotal role in your overall satisfaction and investment success. Research upcoming neighborhoods that align with your lifestyle, considering factors such as proximity to work, local amenities, and community vibes. Stay informed about new developments, as emerging areas may offer opportunities for affordable housing and potential appreciation.

Condos and Homeowners Association (HOA) Fees: If you're looking for a condo, please be sure to keep an eye on the HOA fees. These fees cover shared expenses like maintenance, landscaping, and amenities. While condos often provide a more maintenance-free lifestyle, it's crucial to factor in these additional costs. Please thoroughly review the HOA documents to make sure they align with your preferences and budget.

Avoiding the House-Poor Trap: In the excitement of homeownership, it's easy to get caught up in the allure of a dream home. However, it's essential to strike a balance and avoid the house-poor scenario. Determine a budget that allows for comfortable living while still maintaining financial flexibility. Refrain from stretching yourself thin with a mortgage that leaves little room for you to enjoy life beyond paying bills!

Unlocking Financial Freedom

A Millennial's Guide to Smart Money Moves

Take Your Time and Be Patient: I can't stress taking your time to research and educate yourself enough! Rushing into a home purchase can lead to regrettable decisions. Take your time to research, evaluate, and compare different properties thoroughly. Gather as much information as possible. Patience is your ally in finding the right home that aligns with your financial goals and lifestyle.

Embrace the Long-Term Vision: Homeownership is a long-term commitment, and your chosen property should align with your future aspirations. Consider your plans for the next 5, 10, or even 20 years. Will the home accommodate potential life changes, such as a growing family or a career shift? Will you have to take in aging parents? Ensuring your home meets both current and future needs is integral to a successful homeownership journey.

While government-backed loans and first-time homebuyer programs are essential components of the home-buying process, a comprehensive approach involves discussions with partners, thorough research on locations and property types, and a patient, long-term mindset, incorporating these aspects into your homeownership plan enhances your financial preparedness and sets the stage for a fulfilling and sustainable homeownership experience.

Continuous Learning and Adaptability: The financial landscape and your financial strategies are evolving. Stay informed about market trends, new investment opportunities, and emerging financial technologies. Continuous learning ensures you remain agile in adapting your financial plan to changing circumstances.

Unlocking financial freedom requires commitment, discipline, and continuous learning. Embrace the journey, stay focused on your goals, and watch your financial freedom unfold. Here's to your prosperous and financially liberated future!

04
Soignée

How We Love, Heal & Empower

"How We Love, Heal & Empower" navigates the intricate world of both gay and straight relationships, emphasizing universal themes of love, understanding, and mutual support. This inclusive segment celebrates the uniqueness of each relationship, addressing varied challenges and joys. We aim to foster deeper connections across the love spectrum through stories and expert insights, highlighting the importance of emotional bonding and communication. It's a journey towards a more empathetic, inclusive society where every bond is cherished, and every individual is empowered to love authentically.

UNLOCKING SELF-DISCOVERY

A Path to Healing from Toxic Relationships

HOW WE LOVE & EMPOWER

Unlocking Self-Discovery

Sometimes we have to step out of our comfort zones. We have to break the rules. And we have to discover the sensuality of fear. We need to face it, challenge it, dance with it. —Kyra Davis

The path to healing involves delving into the pieces of oneself that toxic relationships may have obscured. Explore the stories you've told yourself and unveil your truth, strength, and new normal. Engage in self-discovery activities that nurture personal growth, including exploring your sexual needs.

In the aftermath of toxic relationships, a crucial step toward healing is going on a journey of self-discovery. The remnants of these relationships often obscure essential parts of ourselves, and reclaiming our true essence becomes a transformative process. Here's a guide on how to focus on self-discovery:

Unveil Your Truth
↠ Peel back the layers of conditioning and external influences that may have overshadowed your authentic self. Ask yourself probing questions about your needs, values, desires, and dreams. Allow your inner truth to emerge, unfiltered.

↠ Take a moment to reflect on the narratives you've crafted about yourself. Toxic relationships may have distorted your self-perception. Consider your stories about your worth, capabilities, and resilience.

Explore Your Strengths
↠ Toxic relationships often diminish our awareness of our strengths. Make a list of qualities and skills that make you unique. Identify instances in your life where these strengths manifested, reinforcing your sense of power and self-confidence.

Cultivate Resilience
↠ Resilience is a powerful force that can emerge from adversity. Acknowledge the challenges you've faced and conquered. Recognize the inner strength that propelled you forward. Every obstacle navigated is a testament to your resilience.

Engage in Personal Growth Activities
↠ Actively participate in activities that promote personal growth. This could include reading self-help books, attending sensual awakening workshops or therapy sessions, practicing mindfulness, or pursuing hobbies that bring you joy. These activities contribute to your ongoing self-discovery journey.

Journal Your Insights
↠ Keep a journal to document your thoughts, insights, and moments of joy. Writing can be a cathartic process that helps articulate your emotions and track your progress. Revisit your journal to celebrate milestones and reflect on your growth.

Unlocking Self-Discovery

Surround Yourself with Positivity
➤ Cultivate relationships that contribute to your growth and well-being. Building a strong support system is essential for navigating the challenges of creating a new normal after a toxic relationship. Share your goals and aspirations with those who genuinely care about your happiness and success.

Embrace Vulnerability
➤ Prioritize emotional healing! Allow yourself to be vulnerable in the process. Vulnerability is not a sign of weakness but a gateway to authenticity. Embracing vulnerability fosters a deeper connection with yourself and others. Take this opportunity to explore and understand yourself on a deeper level. Allow yourself to feel and express your emotions. Acknowledge the progress you've made and the insights gained. Self-discovery is an ongoing process, and every moment of revelation is a cause for celebration.

Reconnect with Your Body
➤ Engaging in intentional self-exploration opens the door to a more authentic and fulfilling life. Rebuilding a positive relationship with your body involves a holistic approach that encompasses both physical and emotional well-being. After emerging from a toxic relationship, it's common to experience a disconnect between your body and your sense of self. To address this, engaging in activities that promote physical well-being becomes crucial.

Adopting a New Fitness Routine
➤ Introducing a new fitness routine can be transformative in reconnecting with your body. Exercise contributes to physical health and releases endorphins, the "feel-good" hormones that positively impact mood. Choose activities you enjoy, whether it's yoga, pole dancing, hiking, or any exercise that brings joy and increases vitality. The goal is to celebrate what your body can accomplish!

Exploring Sensual and Pleasurable Experiences
➤ Reconnecting with your body also involves exploring sensual and pleasurable experiences in a positive and consensual manner. It's about cultivating a positive relationship with pleasure, ensuring that you can embrace and enjoy these experiences without any guilt or reservations.

➤ Exploring your own sensuality and understanding what brings you pleasure on a personal level can be empowering. This could involve self-exploration with sex toys, learning about your own desires through social groups geared toward adult experiences, and embracing a healthy sense of sexuality as a fully healed woman. The emphasis here is on reclaiming your autonomy and discovering what brings you joy and fulfillment in a way that aligns with your values and comfort. Kick off your heels and dig in!

Combining these elements will nurture your physical health and foster a positive and respectful relationship with your body. This process is about reclaiming ownership of your body, celebrating its uniqueness, and embracing the journey of self-discovery and self-love. Sis, you got this!

EMANCIPATE YOURSELF FROM FEAR'S GRIP

Unlocking the Path to Liberation

HOW WE LOVE & EMPOWER

Embrace Freedom: The Art of Letting Go

The profound act of letting go transforms into a pathway to liberation. With an unwavering commitment to empowering women to shed the burdens of fear, guilt, shame, toxic relationships, and all that no longer serves their soul.

Fear, a stealthy saboteur, often silently keeps us anchored to the familiar. I'm encouraging women to confront their fears, acknowledge them, and then release their hold. Liberation awaits on the other side of fear!

Embrace Freedom: The Art of Letting Go
Take a proactive step to confront and overcome fear by actively seeking unfamiliar experiences or situations. Challenge yourself to step outside your comfort zone; this process will contribute to dismantling the invisible barriers and facilitate personal growth.

Welcome the opportunity for transformation that comes with navigating new pathways and gradually releasing the bonds of fear. Let's explore additional pathways to release the grip:

Mindful Exploration: Engage in mindfulness practices that encourage deep self-reflection. Observing your thoughts and emotions without judgment creates a space to understand the roots of fear. Mindfulness cultivates awareness, empowering you to dismantle fear's stronghold.

Courageous Affirmations: Craft affirmations that resonate with courage. Repeatedly confirm your ability to face and overcome your worries. These positive declarations gradually reshape your mindset, diminishing the power fear holds over your decisions and actions.

Incremental Exposure: Gradually expose yourself to fear-inducing situations in manageable increments. You acclimate your mind and body to the perceived threats by taking small steps, diminishing their potency over time. This progressive approach builds confidence.

Visualize Triumph: Harness the power of visualization to see yourself triumphing over fears. Create mental images of successfully navigating challenging situations. Visualization primes your mind to embrace positive outcomes, reducing the impact of fear on your psyche.

Educate Yourself: Knowledge is a powerful antidote to fear! Dive into learning about the specific fears that grip you. Understanding the underlying causes and dispelling myths can demystify the fear, making it more manageable and less intimidating.

Embrace Freedom: The Art of Letting Go

Shedding the Layers of Guilt and Shame: Self-liberation requires shedding the layers of guilt and shame that weigh down the spirit. These emotions act as heavy garments, constraining authentic self-expression and hindering personal growth.

To unravel these burdens, first, cultivate self-compassion. Recognize that everyone makes mistakes and experiences imperfections; it's a shared human experience.

Second, practice forgiveness—both towards yourself and others. Forgiveness is a powerful tool for liberation, creating a safe space for self-discovery and empowering individuals to embrace their authentic selves without the weight of past missteps.

For women seeking to implement these strategies, start by:
1. Acknowledging and accepting imperfections, understanding they don't define your worth.
2. Practice self-compassion by treating yourself with the same grace you offer others.
3. Releasing the grip of past mistakes and allowing space for personal growth.

You can step into your authentic self with an unburdened spirit, reclaiming your power and living unapologetically. Give yourself permission to let go...I have faith that you can do it!

Breaking Free from Toxic Relationships: Toxic relationships, like anchors, weigh us down and impede our path to peace. Identifying these anchors, acknowledging the toxicity, and gracefully letting go are key aspects of the process. It begins with being truthful with ourselves. What do you really want, and how are you going to get it?

Decluttering Emotional Landscapes: Declutter not just physical spaces but emotional landscapes; this process creates room for clarity and focus; this step clears the emotional canvas, allowing individuals to paint their lives with authenticity and purpose.

The art of letting go transcends a mere act; it becomes a celebration of reclaiming one's authentic self. Through shared stories, expert advice, and a nurturing community, women can discover the strength to release what no longer serves them, paving the way for a life adorned with authenticity, purpose, and boundless joy.

I wish you enough! Cheers to a future unburdened, unbounded, and undeniably extraordinary!

Burnout

"While burnout obviously has something to do with stress, overdoing things, not being centered, and not listening to yourself or your body, one of the deepest contributors to burnout, I believe, is the deep disappointment of not living up to your true calling."
– Jenn Bruer

RENEW
RECHARGE
REVIVE

Burnout

Navigating the intimate space of caregiving, spouses often find themselves entangled in a complex web of emotions, physical exhaustion, and mental strain. Recognizing the imminent threat of burnout is crucial for personal well-being and the ability to provide quality care to a partner grappling with disability or illness.

As the weight of continuous emotional, physical, and mental stress looms, caregiver burnout becomes a real challenge that extends beyond the typical relationship pressures. In order to fortify against these challenges, caregivers must embrace a comprehensive set of coping strategies. These strategies are indispensable for weathering the storm and fostering a resilient and balanced caregiving experience.

In the midst of these challenges, caregivers can discover a profound reservoir of strength within themselves. The journey of caregiving, though demanding, holds the potential for personal growth and deep connections with your spouse or life partner. By acknowledging and addressing burnout head-on, caregivers pave the way for renewal—a process that involves reclaiming their own well-being while continuing to be a pillar of support for their partners.

This exploration into overcoming burnout can be a transformative experience. It is an opportunity for you to delve into the depths of compassion for the partner under care and oneself. Through renewal, recharge, and revival, caregivers can navigate the intricate caregiving landscape with grace and purpose, ensuring that the journey is not only endured but embraced with profound understanding and unwavering strength. Let's look at a few ways to get started:

Empowerment as an Antidote: Taking back control becomes crucial in the battle against burnout for caregivers. It's all about embracing this empowering idea that caregivers can tackle challenges more effectively by reclaiming a sense of control and recognizing their own agency. When we say "antidote," we're really highlighting that embracing empowerment acts as a remedy, actively counteracting the draining impact of feeling powerless or overwhelmed.

Renew, Recharge, Revive
Overcoming Caregiver's Burnout

Empowerment nudges a shift in mindset, creating a safe space for personal resilience. Even when external factors, like time, finances, or assistance, might throw up roadblocks, the ability to boost happiness and nurture hope remains firmly within the caregiver's reach. Picture empowerment as a reliable companion! Every moment becomes a chance for a compassionate adjustment, uncovering bits of solace and joy amid what might seem like overwhelming responsibilities.

Embrace Acceptance - In the face of a loved one's illness or the burdens of caregiving, the pursuit of answers and fairness can drain your energy without yielding relief. Avoid the emotional pitfalls of self-pity or blame; instead, focus on acceptance. Acknowledge the situation, find meaning in your caregiving choice, and unearth positive motivations that fuel your commitment.

Celebrate the significance of every effort, recognizing that you don't have to cure your loved one's illness to make a meaningful impact. Creating an environment of safety, comfort, and love holds profound value. Reflect on the personal growth and strengthened connections that caregiving has afforded you. Uncover the positive aspects that can serve as a source of strength in challenging times.

Preserving Life Beyond Caregiving - Guard against the encroachment of caregiving into every facet of your life. Invest time in areas that provide meaning and purpose, whether it be family, church, hobbies, or your career. A diversified life makes coping with difficult situations more manageable. Organize the chaos! Taming the chaos of caregiving responsibilities involves organizational mastery. Utilize binders for crucial documents, maintain digital information through computer folders, and employ calendars or planners to streamline medical appointments and medication schedules.

Focus on Manageable Task - Break down overwhelming caregiving tasks into manageable chunks. Instead of succumbing to the weight of the entire week's responsibilities, create daily to-do lists and conquer one task at a time. Accept the limitations of wishing for more time or coercing others to contribute more. Shift your focus to *your* reactions in the face of challenges, emphasizing the aspects within *your* control.

Establishing Clear Communication - Open and honest communication is vital for both the caregiver and the spouse or partner receiving care. Establishing clear communication channels can help address concerns, share feelings, and ensure everyone is on the same page. Regular check-ins, both emotionally and practically, can prevent misunderstandings and provide a platform for mutual support.

The coping strategies outlined above become indispensable to fortify against the multifaceted challenges of caregiving. These strategies serve as a toolkit, empowering caregivers to navigate the demanding terrain with resilience and cultivate a healthier balance in their lives.

The acknowledgment and implementation of these coping mechanisms are vital steps towards ensuring not only the well-being of the caregiver but also the provision of quality care to a loved one facing disability or illness. Good luck, and there is no shame in making you a priority!

Power of Pause

Embracing Tranquility

"Growing into your future with health and grace and beauty doesn't have to take all your time. It rather requires a dedication to caring for yourself as if you were rare and precious, which you are, and regarding all life around you as equally so, which it is."

Victoria Moran

Prioritizing Self-Care During Menopause

A Holistic Approach to Well-Being During Menopause

As women navigate the transformative journey of menopause, it becomes imperative to recognize the profound impact that self-care and mindfulness can have on their well-being. Together, they create a harmonious approach to navigating this significant life transition.

The Power of Pause: Prioritizing Self-Care During Menopause
Menopause is a natural phase of a woman's life, signifying the end of her reproductive years. However, the accompanying hormonal changes can bring about a myriad of physical and emotional challenges.

Nurturing the Body: Menopause often brings about physical discomfort, including hot flashes, fatigue, and changes in sleep patterns. Prioritizing self-care involves adopting healthy lifestyle habits such as regular exercise, a balanced diet rich in nutrients, and sufficient hydration. These practices alleviate physical symptoms and contribute to an overall sense of well-being.

Embracing Emotional Well-Being: Menopause can be emotionally taxing, with mood swings and heightened stress levels. Taking the time for self-reflection and engaging in activities that bring joy and relaxation is crucial. Whether it's practicing chakra or vipassana meditation, pursuing hobbies, or spending quality time with loved ones, these moments of pause are essential for maintaining emotional equilibrium.

Mindful Menopause: How Unplugging and Unwinding Can Improve Your Well-Being
Mindfulness is a powerful tool that complements self-care during menopause. It involves being present in the moment, cultivating awareness, and fostering a non-judgmental acceptance of one's experiences.

1. Digital Detox for Mental Clarity
In the age of constant connectivity, women going through menopause may find solace in unplugging from digital devices. The incessant barrage of information and social media can contribute to stress and anxiety. Women can create mental space by intentionally taking breaks from screens, allowing for more profound self-reflection and a calmer mindset.

2. The Art of Unwinding
Menopause can disrupt sleep patterns, exacerbating fatigue and impacting overall well-being. Mindful unwinding techniques, such as deep breathing exercises or gentle yoga, can be transformative. These practices aid in better sleep, help manage stress, and promote a sense of inner calm.

The Synergy of Self-Care and Mindfulness: By integrating the power of pause through self-care practices with the mindfulness of unplugging and unwinding, women can navigate menopause with greater resilience and grace. This synergy allows for a holistic approach to well-being, addressing both the physical and emotional aspects of this transformative life stage.

Menopause is not just a biological event but a profound and individualized journey that deserves attention and care. Embracing the power of pause empowers women to navigate this transition with a sense of control, resilience, and an unwavering commitment to their well-being. As we embrace tranquility during menopause, we discover the strength that comes from honoring ourselves through intentional moments created just for us!

Pause, recharge, and embrace the healing rhythm of your breath. In these moments, rediscover strength and grace.

Your inner restoration unfolds with each inhale, a gentle reminder that self-care is the art of nurturing the soul.

HOLISTIC RECOVERY
Healing, Finances, and Inner Renewal

I pray that you will find solace within this Holistic Guide to Bounce Back from Illness, Fortify Finances, and Rediscover Your Inner Goddess!

So, let's talk about you – the incredible woman who's not just bouncing back from a health setback but ready to thrive in every aspect of her life. This isn't about capes and superhero moves; it's about you, your well-being, and your journey to reclaim control and vibrancy.

Imagine this as your personalized roadmap – not just getting back on your feet, but soaring higher than ever. It's your self-care package, addressing your physical, emotional, and financial well-being. No superhero theatrics, just practical and uplifting steps to bring back the glow in your life.

When we say "holistic," think of it as your Soignée toolkit for self-improvement – fixing what needs attention both inside and out. It's acknowledging that your health, emotions, and finances are intertwined, and we're here to nurture each aspect simultaneously!

HOLISTIC RECOVERY
Healing, Finances, and Inner Renewal

For some, recovery means delving into the sacred domains of your inner goddess—a unique and profound aspect of your being that radiates strength, resilience, and untapped potential. Unlike any exploration mentioned before, this journey is about unveiling the mystical layers within you and embracing the extraordinary essence that sets you aglow.

Soulful Connection with Nature: Commune with the natural world to ignite your inner goddess. Take solitary walks in the woods, allowing the rustling leaves and gentle breezes to reconnect you with the primal, untouched energy within.

Dance of Liberation: Engage in the ancient art of dance as a form of self-liberation. Allow your body to move freely, expressing the unspoken desires and passions that reside within. This dance isn't about perfection but the raw and unfiltered celebration of your true self.

Sacred Sound Bath: Immerse yourself in the healing vibrations of a sound bath. Whether through chanting, singing bowls, or resonant music, let the harmonious frequencies penetrate your soul, awakening dormant aspects of your inner goddess.

Meditative Mandala Coloring Books: Visit Amazon and purchase an intricate mandala coloring book for adults to use as a meditative practice. Each stroke and pattern you create becomes a visual representation of the inner peace within you.

Goddess Affirmations: Craft affirmations that resonate with your divine essence. Repeat these affirmations daily, allowing their empowering energy to permeate your consciousness. These affirmations become mantras, guiding you towards self-love and acceptance.

Moonlit Contemplation: Bask in the moon's gentle glow during quiet evenings. Let the lunar energy infuse you with intuitive wisdom and emotional clarity. Moonlit contemplation becomes a sacred dialogue between you and the celestial forces guiding your inner goddess.

Rituals of Self-Adoration: Develop personal rituals that honor and cherish your body, mind, and spirit. They could include nurturing skincare routines, aromatic baths, or mindful self-massage. The intention is to treat yourself as the goddess you are.

HOLISTIC RECOVERY
Healing, Finances, and Inner Renewal

Awakening your inner goddess is a sacred quest, a journey beyond the mundane and into the extraordinary. As you embrace these unique explorations, envision your inner goddess as a luminous force, casting a radiant glow upon every step of your recovery journey. It's not merely about bouncing back; it's about ascending into the divine masterpiece that is you.

Your recovery isn't a dance floor, but let's call it a journey of rhythm – where your physical, emotional, and financial steps harmonize. Because, let's be real, life isn't a stage; it's a journey, and you're the star!

Let's kick off by prioritizing your health, focusing on activities that won't break the bank. There are no magic potions here; consider working on a tailored diet with insights from a nutritionist. Also, try these websites for more resources: www.eatright.org and www.nutrition.gov

Embrace low-impact exercises, not for a superhero cape effect, but to ensure you heal gracefully. Develop a personalized exercise plan with a local gym trainer, ensuring every step is gentle and comfortable. Don't forget YouTube tutorials!

Now, for activities that bring peace and well-being without spending a dime:

Mindful Meditation: Dedicate some time each day to mindful meditation. Find a quiet space, sit comfortably, and focus on your breath. It's a cost-free way to cultivate inner peace.

Nature Walks: Explore nearby parks or nature trails. Connecting with nature has a calming effect on the mind and body. Take in the fresh air and enjoy the beauty around you.

Journaling: Dive into the joy of journaling by joining a lively Facebook club or kickstart your Zoom meetup! Picture this: a virtual space buzzing with creative energy where you and fellow journal enthusiasts come together to share thoughts and experiences. Grab your favorite pen, find a comfy spot, and let the journaling party begin! And hey, why stop there? Explore other expressive avenues like creating a Pinterest board for your journaling inspiration or exchanging voice messages with your newfound journaling pals. The possibilities are as limitless as your imagination!

Creative Outlets: Engage in creative activities like drawing, writing, or crafting. You don't need fancy materials – use what you have at home to explore your artistic side.

Online Resources: Unlock a world of well-being with a plethora of online resources that won't cost you a dime!

Dive into guided yoga or dance sessions available on various platforms such as YouTube, offering complimentary sessions to elevate your well-being journey. But wait, there's more!

Spice up your routine by exploring free cooking classes online, teaching others your favorite recipes, or joining virtual dance parties to get your body moving with joy.

Why not embark on a new skill with free language-learning apps or start a mentorship to share your wisdom?

Feeling community-driven? Create a virtual church ministry program or initiate a book club to connect with like-minded souls. The online world is your oyster, brimming with innovative ways to nurture your mind, body, and spirit without spending a penny!

Your well-being is a priority, and there are numerous activities that can contribute to your peace and healing without putting a strain on your finances!

Talk it out, explore those feelings, and transform the emotional ride into a smooth journey. Seeking support through counseling or therapy is like having a trusted guide through your emotional landfill during recovery.

Financial superhero moves: It's not about you becoming a rescue mission! You can assess your finances, sell those goodies, and explore some remote work opportunities.

Healing, Finances, and Inner Renewal

Now, let's dive deeper into building financial stability. Think of it as a financial cha-cha, ensuring your money moves are not just stable but graceful.

Step 1: Assess Your Financial Situation Meticulously
This isn't about crunching numbers but understanding your financial landscape. Identify debts – categorize them based on interest rates, outstanding balances, and due dates. Prioritize essential expenses – what are the non-negotiables? Create a realistic budget – factor in necessary costs like utilities, groceries, insurance, and debt repayments. This detailed assessment forms the foundation of your financial recovery.

Step 2: The Elegant Twist – Liquidate Assets Strategically
Here's the elegant twist in your financial dance – liquidate assets that are no longer essential. Look around your space; what items have served their purpose or don't align with your current needs? It could be unused electronics, furniture, or other items with resale value. Selling these assets declutters your space and injects immediate funds into your financial recovery plan.

Consider online platforms like eBay, Facebook Marketplace, or specialized selling apps. Check out Poshmark, ThredUp, Kidizen, and VarageSale to sell clothes! This isn't just about making money; it's about optimizing your resources and ensuring every asset contributes to your financial well-being.

Step 3: Embrace Remote Work Opportunities
In today's dynamic work landscape, remote opportunities abound. Explore platforms like Upwork or Freelancer, where your skills can shine without the confines of a traditional office. Leverage your expertise, whether it's in writing, graphic design, consulting, or any other field. This isn't just about making ends meet; it's about redefining your work-life balance on your terms.

Step 4: Seek Financial Guidance
Your financial journey deserves an expert touch. Consult with a financial advisor who can provide personalized guidance on debt management, budgeting, and investment strategies. This is about crafting a financial plan that aligns with your goals and aspirations.

Now, let's weave these steps seamlessly into your journey of holistic recovery, where every move contributes to your thriving and flourishing. See, this journey is not about bouncing *back*; it's about bouncing *forward* into your most fabulous, fierce, and fulfilled self!

No superhero capes, just your inner strength. So, please put on your metaphorical power suit, gather your wisdom, and let's rock this holistic recovery journey! You've got this!

05 Soignée

Soignée Soul After Dark

Soignée Soul After Dark, a personal retreat, takes place over the course of 60 minutes, during which you are guided through a series of immersive activities carefully designed to promote relaxation and introspection. Soignée Soul paves the way for a deeper understanding of self and a renewed commitment to holistic well-being by inviting you to explore mindful practices, creative expression, and communal connections.

Soignee Soul After Dark: A Sacred Space for Women

Soignee Soul After Dark was created for women in search of solace and rejuvenation, offering a sacred, quiet space to reset and recharge amid the tumult of daily life. The newsletter serves as your exclusive retreat—a refuge for personal development, healing, and the fearless exploration of one's true self. Join us on a transformative journey as we champion the potency of self-care, nurture individual growth, and honor the audacity it takes to remain authentic, even if it necessitates bidding farewell to some along the way.

Come join our empowering newsletter and community as we bask in the empowering influence of journaling. Together, let's illuminate the path of authenticity, recognizing that sometimes, bidding farewell is the inaugural step toward embracing the extraordinary journey that awaits. Here's to fearlessly pursuing the essence of your true self beneath the moonlit canopy of Soignee After Dark!

We seek to elevate your confidence with daily affirmations, sustain your commitment through accountability posts, and become part of a nurturing series dedicated to growth. Unearth your inner wisdom through daily reflection, nurture a positive mindset, prioritize self-care, and welcome profound personal growth with open arms.

Confidence Amplification - Elevate your self-assurance through the ritual of daily affirmations, fortifying an unwavering foundation for your journey towards flourishing.

Commitment Fortification - Ensure enduring transformations by tethering yourself to commitment through meticulously crafted accountability texts tailored to your aspirations.

Empowering Collective - Immerse yourself in the sanctuary of our online community—a bastion of support, fostering shared growth and knowledge in the dynamic tapestry of contemporary society.

Wisdom Unveiling - Illuminate the corridors of your inner wisdom with the artistry of daily self-reflection prompts, a compass guiding you through the labyrinth of clarity.

Mindset Alchemy - Engage in the cultivation of a compelling positive mindset, a magnetic force drawing love, success, and happiness into the evolving narrative of your life.

Self-Care Symphony - Articulate the melody of self-care, harmonizing the notes of well-being, and embrace a profound path to personal growth, unlocking the latent facets of your true potential.

Envision the nightly retreats ahead filled with whispered wisdom and the gentle glow of self-discovery. May you find solace in the pages of Soignee After Dark, and may each word be a reminder that your resilience is a force to be celebrated! Let personal growth blossom, healing unfold, and the courage to be authentically you fill your pages.

Sign up for the newsletter or scan the QR code: https://bit.ly/3PLg1cb

Your presence will not only be acknowledged but celebrated! Here's to a month of empowerment, enlightenment, and the beauty of being unapologetically you. Enjoy the transformative journey!

Scan Me to Learn More

Using Soignée Soul After Dark

Here are fabulous ways you can make the most of this transformative experience.

01   **Lose Yourself in the Retreat Experience**: During the 60-minute retreat, let go of the outside world. Create a serene space, light a candle, pour your favorite beverage, put on your most sensual gown, turn on soothing music, and immerse yourself fully. Follow the guided activities from the newsletter with an open heart. This is your time to reconnect with yourself on a profound level. Be present, be gentle with yourself, and allow the retreat to weave its magic. As you use the journal prompts and affirmations, be true to you!

02   **Craft Your Creative Expression**: Unleash your creativity through the immersive activities designed just for you. Let your inner artist emerge, whether it's writing poetry or a song, doodling, painting, writing, or any other form of expression. This is your time to explore the beauty of creation without judgment. Expressing yourself creatively is a powerful way to tap into your inner wisdom and unveil the authentic you.

03   **Connect with the Community**: Our Crown Holders Sisterhood community is an online sisterhood of like-minded souls, and you can become a cherished part of it. Engage with fellow retreat participants. Share your thoughts, experiences, and aspirations. You'll find support, encouragement, and perhaps lifelong friends who understand your journey. In the CHS community, you are never alone. Let's uplift each other and grow together.

04   **Escape with the YouTube Mental Retreat Series**: Transport yourself to a serene mental oasis with our YouTube Mental Escape Series. Close your eyes, breathe deeply, and let the calming visuals and sounds wash away the stresses of the day. It's a mini-vacation for your mind. Use these retreats whenever you need a moment of tranquility – your personal escape hatch to serenity.

Immerse Yourself in the Podcast: Tune into our soul-nourishing podcast. Let the soothing voices and enlightening conversations wash over you. As you go about your day, whether commuting, cooking or simply relaxing, absorb the empowering stories and wisdom shared by incredible women. It's like having a heart-to-heart chat with your best friend – comforting, inspiring, and always there when you need it.

Unleashing Your Inner Badass
On the Road to Self-Healing

Self-healing from emotional and physical wounds demands a no-nonsense approach to shedding the weight of guilt and shame. No more tiptoeing – it's time to kick those burdens to the curb! Navigating the intricate terrain of human consciousness involves tackling overt and subtle self-criticism. Together, let's recognize and dismantle these ingrained patterns, taking the initial steps toward a profound transformation that leads to a lighter, more peaceful existence. You're not alone–we are here to support you every step of the way!

Consider the reluctance to accept compliments or the persistent desire to outdo one's achievements gracefully – these subtle signs reveal self-critical tendencies that hinder personal growth and overall well-being.

Moments of frustration at our vulnerabilities echo a learned habit of being unkind to oneself. Acknowledging this self-inflicted negativity is crucial, as it consumes precious time and energy that could be redirected toward positive endeavors.

Unleashing Your Inner Badass On the Road to Self-Healing

Breaking free from this cycle of self-criticism becomes imperative for genuine emotional and physical healing. Speaking our truth is a powerful act aligning us with the flow of life, involving a willingness to risk potential rejection as we navigate the uncertain waters of authenticity. The remnants of past experiences, where others made us feel inadequate, linger in our bodies, creating discomfort. Embracing the truth, even when uncomfortable, is integral to self-acceptance and healing.

Life's path is only sometimes clearly defined, requiring us to follow our choices to their logical conclusions. As we commit to living and speaking our truth, even in the face of potential rejection, we open ourselves up to the supportive currents of life, enabling us to channel our energy into cultivating well-being on all levels.

Honoring the truth in every interaction becomes a transformative choice. We can make honesty the cornerstone of our existence, inviting the nurturing power of the universe's energy into our lives! This choice aligns us with positive, lasting results, creating a harmonious inner landscape. The willingness to speak our truth is empowering, allowing us to use our energy to shape our dreams rather than draining ourselves with falsehoods.

Breaking free from the shackles of self-imposed guilt requires a conscious effort to reevaluate past choices in a constructive light. Learning to accept perceived wrongs can be challenging, especially when societal norms dictate that guilt is a necessary emotion for rectifying past actions. However, shifting towards healthier coping mechanisms, such as forgiveness and understanding, proves more beneficial.

Overcoming being hard on oneself is akin to breaking any other stubborn habit. Recognizing the burden it places on our overall well-being serves as motivation for change. Initially, mere awareness of self-critical moments is sufficient. As this awareness grows, an intrinsic drive towards health and well-being is activated, steering us towards a more positive and natural relationship with ourselves.

Retrospection of our past actions unveils multiple dimensions of our behavior. While guilt may provide momentary relief, it is merely a superficial remedy. Proper understanding emerges when we approach our past with compassion. Our actions were attempts to protect ourselves or others, made under the constraints of the moment. Embracing this perspective but letting it go allows us to move beyond negative feelings and embark on a journey of self-forgiveness, a crucial step in genuine healing.

Permitting ourselves to find peace with past actions is a pivotal stride towards a life free from regrets and guilt. Realizing true tranquility stems from accepting every facet of our existence and propels us towards inner harmony and joy. By fostering a therapeutic approach centered on self-compassion, acceptance, and forgiveness, we pave the way for a transformative healing process that extends into all aspects of our lives.

The journey towards healing from emotional and physical abuse is nuanced and requires releasing guilt and shame, which demands a conscious effort to break free from the cycle of self-criticism and acknowledge the subtle ways we undermine our well-being.

Today, as we choose honesty in every interaction, we invite the nurturing power of the universe's energy, bringing about positive, lasting results in all aspects of our lives.

Self Adore

In the sensual journey of self-adore, I unearth the depths of my desires and passions. Each heartbeat resonates with self-love, nurturing authenticity and igniting a fiery sensuality that sets my spirit ablaze.

EMBRACING YOUR BEAUTIFUL IMPERFECTIONS

Confidence is a journey, not a destination. Instead of fixating on achieving a certain standard, work on becoming fully confident in your body as it is right now. Celebrate the strength, resilience, and uniqueness that define you. Confidence is not about conforming; it's about embracing your individuality and walking your path with pride.

Acceptance is a lifelong practice that extends to all ages and stages of your life. To actively cultivate acceptance, start by practicing gratitude for your body. Create a ritual of appreciation, acknowledging the unique qualities and strengths each phase of life brings. Surround yourself with positive influences and engage in activities that uplift and inspire you. Seek out role models who exude self-confidence at every age and stage, reminding yourself that beauty is not confined by societal standards.

In the pursuit of self-love, remember that the *journey* is as important as the *destination*. Embrace your beautiful imperfections! Your body is a masterpiece, a reflection of your strength and the love you carry within. It's time to let that love shine!

Incorporating a routine of appreciation into your daily life is a personal journey that starts with recognizing and valuing the uniqueness of your body. Take a few moments each day to stand in front of the mirror and consciously acknowledge the qualities and strengths that each phase of your life has brought forth. Whether it's the resilience you've shown during challenging times or the changes that reflect the passage of time, intentionally express gratitude for these aspects.

Surround yourself with positivity by curating your environment to include sources of inspiration and encouragement. This could involve connecting with like-minded individuals, engaging in activities that bring you joy, or simply immersing yourself in uplifting content. Find what resonates with you personally and makes you feel empowered.

Consider keeping a journal where you document daily moments of self-appreciation and achievements. Reflecting on these entries over time can serve as a tangible reminder of your growth and the strengths you possess.

Developing a routine of appreciation is about customizing practices that align with your unique journey, making it a personal and meaningful part of your self-acceptance process. You can infuse intention into each moment of appreciation, making it a powerful component of your self-acceptance journey. You are beautiful, and it's time you own it!

EMBRACING YOUR BEAUTIFUL IMPERFECTIONS

Ladies, it's high time we seize our inner strength and fully embrace the love we deserve for ourselves. Let's own our bodies, flaws and all, with hearts wide open. Real empowerment kicks in when we dive into the profound journey of soul work, going beyond the surface and tapping into the very essence of who we are. Let's take charge and make self-love our superpower!

Healing your body starts with healing your soul. Rather than succumbing to societal pressures that dictate a narrow definition of beauty, focus on nurturing your inner self. Explore the depths of your emotions, acknowledging the wounds that societal expectations or personal struggles may have inflicted. Embrace self-compassion, recognizing that your worth extends far beyond external appearances.

Body shame is a heavy burden that many women carry, often fueled by social media, reality TV portrayals, or hurtful comments. It's essential to release the shackles of shame to liberate yourself from this weight. Acknowledge that your body is uniquely yours, a vessel that has weathered storms and embraced joys. Understand that imperfections are not flaws but unique features that tell your personal story!

For those who have faced bullying or navigate life with disabilities causing depression, the journey to self-love may be more challenging, but it is equally profound. Seek support from those who uplift and cherish you for who you are. Surround yourself with a community that understands the value of diversity and individuality. Healing often requires a combination of professional help and self-reflection, with therapy providing a safe space to explore the emotional toll of past traumas.

The relentless pursuit of validation from others can be exhausting and detrimental to our mental well-being. Release the need for external approval and validation and cultivate a sense of self-worth that comes from within. Authenticity is magnetic, and when you embrace your true self, you radiate a unique beauty that transcends societal expectations!

Renewed sexuality is a natural byproduct of self-acceptance. Begin by setting aside moments of intentional self-reflection. Explore your body with curiosity, without the burden of judgment. Consider engaging in practices to reconnect with your sensuality.

Take small steps to prioritize self-care, whether through nurturing activities, sensual experiences, or exploring your desires safely and consensually. Embrace the idea that your body is a sanctuary of pleasure and empowerment, allowing yourself to experience intimacy without reservations or shame.

> The woman who doesn't require validation from anyone is the most feared individual on the planet.
>
> —Mohadesa Najumi

Soignée Soul Check-ins

This dedicated space within our magazine is much more than a simple check-in. It's a heartfelt embrace, a moment of connection with your inner self, and a celebration of the journey that you, as a Soignée Sister, are on.

These sessions are crafted to inspire, uplift, and resonate deeply with the unique experiences of women of color.

As you pause and reflect on these thoughtful prompts, consider them as gentle reminders to honor your strength, cherish your journey, and embrace your individuality.

Let these sessions be your personal sanctuary, where you can recharge, reflect, and reaffirm the beauty of being you.

So, take a moment, breathe deep, and let's embark on this journey of self-discovery and affirmation together."

This is Just a Moment in Time

"Love yourself through it. Realize that you're doing the best you can right now. Be open to improvising here and there, as necessary.

Release any unhealthy relationship with being in total control. We're being reminded that we're not in control at the end of the day."

– Lalah Delia, author and founder of Vibrate Higher Daily.

SOIGNÉE SOUL JOURNAL PROMPTS

➛ Fostering Self-Love
In what ways do you practice self-love in your daily life? How can cultivating self-love positively impact your mental, spiritual, and physical well-being?

➛ Dismantling Doubts
What doubts or self-limiting beliefs do you currently grapple with? How might you challenge and dismantle these doubts to pave the way for personal growth?

➛ Tapping into Shared Strength
How can you actively contribute to the shared strength of the sisterhood? In what ways can tapping into collective wisdom enhance your individual journey toward authenticity and healing?

➛ Pursuit of Authenticity
Reflect on moments when you felt most authentic. What elements contributed to that authenticity? How does embracing authenticity align with your overall sense of well-being?

➛ Healing Journey
Consider areas in your life that may benefit from healing. What steps can you take to initiate this healing process? How does prioritizing mental, spiritual, and physical well-being contribute to a holistic journey of healing?

➛ Readiness to Tap into Power
What steps are you prepared to take to tap into your personal power? How does the idea of a collective journey toward empowerment resonate with your current aspirations and goals?

Feel free to reflect on these questions individually or share them with your Soignée Sisters as conversation starters within the community.

Soignée Soul Check-ins

When you take care of yourself, you're a better person for others. When you feel good about yourself, you treat others better.—Solange Knowles

1. Acknowledging Every Victory
Pause for a moment and reflect on your achievements. How often do you acknowledge your own successes? Remember, every small victory is a step forward. Honor these triumphs.

2. Celebrate Your Tenacity
Consider the last time you truly celebrated yourself. Have you given yourself credit for the resilience and strength you've shown? Today, take a moment to rejoice in the person you're becoming.

3. Compassion Begins Within
When did you last treat yourself with the same compassion you offered others? Self-love is the wellspring of your strength. Today, be as kind to yourself as you would be to your dearest friend.

4. Empowerment Through Words
Reflect on the power of your voice. Your words can inspire, heal, and empower. Are you using your voice to uplift yourself as you do for others? Your words can be your own source of inspiration.

5. Straighten Your Crown
Think about the crowning moments. You wear an invisible crown shaped by your experiences and wisdom. Today, straighten that crown and walk with the pride that comes from knowing your worth.

Begin by finding a quiet space for introspection. As you engage with each session, allow the prompts to guide you in reflecting on your unique journey. Embrace these moments as opportunities to connect with your inner self, celebrating your strength and individuality. A journal is an excellent tool to document your feelings!

Soignée Soul Check-ins

When I dare to be powerful — to use my strength in the service of my vision, then it becomes less and less important whether I am afraid.
—Audre Lorde, Writer, Womanist, Librarian, and Civil Rights Activist

6. Appreciate Your Fortitude
Contemplate the hurdles you've overcome. Have you taken the time to appreciate your own resilience? Allow yourself to feel pride in your perseverance and the strength that resides within you

7. Celebrate Courageous Steps
Ask yourself when you last stepped outside of your comfort zone for your own growth. Cherishing your courage to face the unknown is a testament to your evolving spirit. Celebrate these bold steps.

8. Reflecting Inner Beauty
When did you last look in the mirror and truly see the beauty and wisdom reflected there? You are a temple of unique experiences, strength and crowned with grace. Honor your unique beauty.

9. Empower Your Spirit
Recall the times you've lifted others. Your ability to empower those around you is a gift. Have you taken the time to empower yourself with the same enthusiasm? Your spirit deserves that same energy.

10. Listen to Your Heart
In the quiet moments, have you listened to your own heart? Your desires, dreams, and aspirations are the melodies of your soul. Allow yourself the space to hear them and the courage to pursue them.

Use these sessions as a sanctuary for recharging and affirming your personal beauty and journey. Remember to breathe deeply and embrace this journey of self-discovery and affirmation. You can find our line of journals here - **https://amzn.to/3ImzcWP**

Be the Magic

"I prefer to be true to myself, even at the hazard of incurring the ridicule of others, rather than to be false, and incur my own abhorrence."

— Frederick Douglass, Narrative of the Life of Frederick Douglass

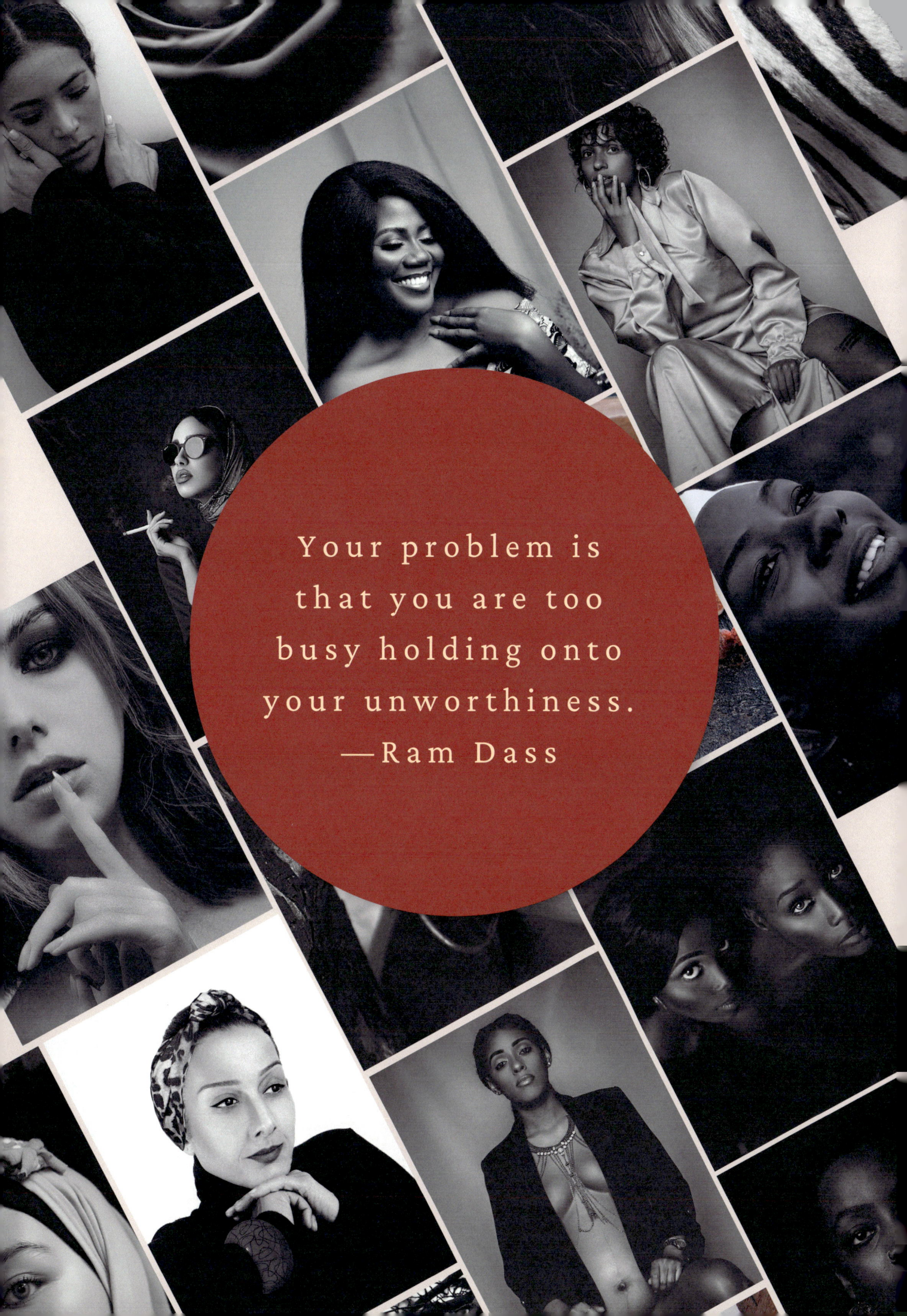

Your problem is that you are too busy holding onto your unworthiness.
—Ram Dass

Connect Beyond the Pages!

As we close the final spread of Soignée Lifestyle Magazine, we invite you to extend the experience into your daily life. Our magazine offers a living, breathing community shaped by the threads of your stories, insights, and shared experiences. We welcome your reviews and would love to share!

Show Your Support Online
Step into the digital realm with us! Follow our adventures, engage in conversations, and be the first to know about exciting updates.

Scan the QR codes provided and follow us on TikTok, Instagram, Twitter, and Facebook. Your virtual presence amplifies the heartbeat of our community.

Let EDC Creations Tell Your Story!

"When we deny our stories, they define us. When we own our stories, we get to write a brave new ending."
—Brené Brown

BAN Radio Show offers a diverse group of international authors a chance to showcase their books to thousands of readers weekly.

Black Pearls Magazine is an award-winning (AALAS x 4) online literary destination for book clubs and thousands of social network fans around the globe.

Let us implement your vision! We can become your virtual assistants to oversee the implementation of your product launch, marketing, and publicity plans.

Scan the QR code to explore the home of EDC Creations Media Group. Let us become part of your team and elevate your dreams.

Explore our services at edc-creations.com

BAN Radio Show

Black Pearls Magazine

Connect Beyond the Pages!

Stay in the Loop – Subscribe Now

Elevate your experience by subscribing to our newsletter. Receive exclusive content, behind-the-scenes glimpses, and special offers. Your inbox is your gateway to a world where possibilities know no bounds. Scan the QR code to subscribe.

Your Stage, Your Story

Calling all trailblazers and event planners! We yearn to witness the power of your stories on a live stage. Invite us to your events, and let's create memories that resonate beyond these pages. Your workshops, conferences, meetups, and unique perspectives will shape the pulse of our future.

Lift Every Voice

Soignée is open to your contributions. We welcome your authentic voice, whether it's articles, poems, or personal stories. Send your submissions to this email address, elladcurry@edc-creations.com and become part of the creative network driving our content. More submission details on our website.

Connect Beyond the Pages!

Gift the Experience

Spread the Soignée magic by gifting a digital copy to someone special. Order online and provide the recipient's email address. They will receive the magazine directly in their inbox as an ebook. It's a thoughtful gesture that shares the celebration of diversity and empowerment.

Support Our Growth

Engage with us on social media! Like, share, comment - be an integral part of our dynamic community. Your participation fuels the growth of our magazine and our online community, and together, we celebrate the beauty of sisterhood.

Order Your Copies

Want to take the experience offline? Scan the QR codes on the next page to order journals, featured books, and digital magazines or purchase printed magazine copies on Amazon. Whether in hand or on screen, Soignée is ready to accompany you. Remember us when giving gifts of love!

Connect Beyond the Pages!

Soignée Soul After Dark: Your Personal Retreat
Escape the hustle and bustle, and join us for Soignée Soul After Dark – a personal retreat designed for you to reset, recharge, and unwind. In just 60 minutes each night, immerse yourself in a sanctuary of tranquility as we guide you through a journey of self-discovery and rejuvenation.

Reset, Recharge, Unwind: Soignée Soul After Dark
Take the first step towards a more balanced and harmonious life. Soignée Soul After Dark invites you to embrace the serenity of each night, dedicating 60 minutes to your well-being. Join us on this journey of self-discovery, and let the magic of our personal retreats unfold. Your sanctuary awaits.

As we bid adieu to this issue, carry the spirit of Soignée with you. Seize this invitation to explore, engage, and actively contribute to the ongoing narrative. Connect beyond the pages, and let's continue this adventure together!

Soignée Soul	TikTok	Facebook
Instagram	Twitter	Pinterest

Connect Beyond the Pages!

Scan the QR Codes to Shop and Explore Our Network

Subscribe to Newsletter

Subscribe to Magazine

Advertise with Us

Soignée Main Website

Crown Holders Website

EDC Creations Website

Black Pearls Magazine

Journals & Planners

She Speaks Truth Bundle

Connect with Ella

Available for keynote addresses, moderating events, and participating in panel discussions or podcasts.

Email Ella D. Curry at elladcurry@edc-creations.com

Showcase Your Gifts

Advertise your book, business or service with Crown Holders Transmedia and EDC Creations Group. Visit our website for investment rates.

Explore EDC Partnership packages at www.edc-creations.com

EDC CREATIONS MEDIA GROUP

Experience the Future of Book Promotion with EDC Creations and Crown Holders Transmedia!

On the forefront of marketing and promotion, EDC Creations, in collaboration with Crown Holders Transmedia and esteemed partners, proudly offers authors an unparalleled array of Web 3.0 services.

At the helm is Ella D. Curry, the visionary owner, who has dedicated years to studying, researching, and cultivating relationships with publishing industry professionals. Beyond industry connections, Ella has forged a unique bond with the bedrock of the publishing world—the avid readers.

While our expansion has broadened the scope of our services and garnered recognition, our driving force remains unwavering. It's a commitment to enhancing literacy, establishing our clients as leaders, and expanding the literary territory for each author we champion.

A 360-degree view of the industry comes effortlessly to us, courtesy of Ella D. Curry's diverse experience. From being a bookstore buyer for the legendary Karibu Books chain to serving as a literary director for A Good Books independent bookstore, an award-winning Internet radio host, digital magazine publisher, corporate event planner, and an avid reader for 35 years—Ella's multifaceted background infuses our approach with unparalleled insights and expertise. Join us in shaping the future of literary promotion!

JOIN OUR COMMUNITY!

We are a family of Reviewers, Authors, Store Owners, Book Clubs, BookTubers, BookTokers and Bookstagrammers!

Tantalizing stories, memorable characters, and provocative storylines are all here at Crown Holders Transmedia!

Step into our digital corridors, where the allure of the written word mingles with the enchantment of visual storytelling and the harmony of soul-stirring melodies.

Crafted by the most gifted artists, authors, writers, and poets on our planet, we proudly present the crème de la crème—the BEST of the BEST! You've just entered a realm where literary brilliance and artistic excellence converge.

Crown Holders Transmedia and EDC Creations Media Group have undergone a transformative journey, evolving from a one-person event planning operation into one of the nation's leading African American woman-owned Internet publicity and book promotion firms.

Visit Crown Holders Transmedia
http://crownholderstransmedia.com

Scan and Shop

Scan any QR codes in this magazine for more information and to purchase any of the books featured in this issue.

Timeless Values in a Modern World

A Soignée Woman is a harmonious blend of external elegance and internal substance. Her values, principles, and overall demeanor set her apart as a symbol of sophistication and refinement in today's diverse and dynamic world.

Made in the USA
Columbia, SC
04 May 2024